★ TOPP COUNTRY ★

A culinary journey

THROUGH NEW ZEALAND WITH THE

Topp Twins

Diva

First published in 2018 by Diva Books
A division of Diva Productions Ltd
PO Box 5986, Wellesley St,
Auckland 1141, New Zealand
Enquiries: info@divaproductions.co.nz

Text: © Arani Cuthbert and Jools Topp
Song lyrics and Ken poems © The Topp Twins
Photography: Cover photo and pages 4 & 11
© Sally Tagg/Woman's Day
All other photography credits: page 259

A catalogue record for this book is available
from the National Library of New Zealand.

ISBN 978-0-473-44297-2
Printed by 1010 Printing

TOPP COUNTRY
IS DEDICATED TO
A TOPP FAMILY

To our wonderful parents
Jean and Peter and
our darling brother Bruce.
Thanks for all the family
meals and stories shared at
the kitchen table.

All our love forever.

Jools and Lynda
(A couple of Dames)

JSTORY www.storyco.kr MADE IN KOREA

FOR THE LOVE OF

PORK   14
LORD & LADY HAVOC,
A SPANISH NZ LOVE STORY,
PIG IN A DAY

SHEEP   30
THE HARMER FAMILY,
THE GREAT NZ SHEEP RESCUE,
KINGSMEADE SHEEP CHEESE

SALMON   44
HIGH COUNTRY SALMON,
RAKAIA SALMON FISHING,
FRANK & HILMA

VENISON   56
FARMED VENISON, WILD VENISON,
BARRYTOWN KNIFEMAKING

GARDEN   68
HOME GARDEN, TE MATA FIGS,
KELMARNA GARDENS

SEA   78
FLEUR'S, WAKA,
TERRAZA SAFFRON

BEEF   92
ANGUS BEEF, THE BUTCHER'S PIES,
LUCKY TACO

POULTRY 106

THE CROZIERS, ANNIE GUINNESS,
A RARE BREED

HERITAGE 116

NEW ZEALAND GAME BIRDS,
THE BOWMANS,
SYMES HONEY

TOPPS 124

TOPP FAMILY, JOOLS TOPP,
LYNDA TOPP

CAMP MOTHER'S SAUCY TIPS 132

GOATS 140

WILD GOAT, THREE LITTLE BIRDS,
KAIKOURA CHEESE

FRUIT 150

COUNTRY TRADING COMPANY,
SUSTAINABLE LIVING & BLUEBERRIES,
LOTHLORIEN FEIJOAS

EXOTIC 160

KOWHAI GROVE OSTRICH FARM,
WHANGARIPO BUFFALO, GRASSHOPPERS

FOR THE LOVE OF

SPICE   **170**
FIRE DRAGON CHILLIES,
ORIENTAL SPICE, TURMERIC

FLOWERS   **184**
LAVENDER, WILD FLOWERS,
TASMAN BAY ROSES

BREAD   **194**
CHALLAH BREAD, MĀORI FRY BREAD

BACKYARD   **204**
KAWHIA HARBOUR,
THE BACKYARD BOYS, MOLESWORTH

ORGANICS   **218**
ORGANIC VEGGIES,
ORGANIC SEAWEED, ORGANIC DAIRY

BUSH   **228**
BUSH FOOD, HURUNUI JACKS LUXURY
GLAMPING, THE WKIWI BUSHMAN

DECADENCE   **238**
OAKLAND TRUFFIERE, CRAYFISH,
CHOCOLATE

TASTY TREATS   **248**
WITH THE BOWLING LADIES

RECIPE INDEX   **256**

FOREWORD
BY COLIN HOGG

When I first knew the Topp Twins, it was the last century and they were living round the corner from me in Grey Lynn. You could spot their place by the tractor parked outside. They were never city slickers though. And they were always aware that the best eats weren't to be had at a pricey place up on Ponsonby Road.

I remember once, when they were visiting my place, the ice-cream truck came down the road playing its child-alerting tune, parking outside and setting my kids shaking me for money. One of the Topps, Lynda I think, put down her cup of tea and said to me, "You don't want to be buying the nippers that stuff Col. It's made out of petrol." So they were onto what's good to put in your mouth even way back then, at the beginning of their extraordinary time with us.

But Dames Jools and Lynda were born extraordinary. Like just a tiny handful of other people we call entertainers, the Topps make you – and certainly me – feel better just by being, even when they're not quite being themselves, but morphing into Camp Mother, Camp Leader, the Bowling Ladies or the manly (and surprisingly poetic) Kens, all of whom feature in this sumptuous and disturbingly scrumptious book.

Aside from several other things – like being hilarious and having sibling harmonies to frighten the Everly Brothers – the Topps are inventive. They've evolved over the years since the 1980s when they pretty much exploded onto the scene after finding their first audience with the women's movement and swiftly moving on to inhabit the nation's hearts and laughing parts.

And, as mentioned, they're inventive, changing without really changing. They can be blokes or go all campy. They can yodel to tingle your nape and still be the Topp Twins, mainly because they can't help but be themselves. So I wasn't in the least surprised when, four or five years ago, Jools and Lynda popped back onto the telly slightly reinvented as roving foodies in a series called *Topp Country*.

Starting out with a chapter called For the Love of Pork, a crackling good yarn about pigs and how cute and tasty they are, the girls wove a good-looking, good-humoured spell travelling the country looking for the hows, whos and wheres of the various things we like to eat.

Each episode was a loving appreciation with recipes, poems, songs and inside stories on the good people who grow and harvest our fave grub. Lambs, salmon, deer, fish, cattle, goats and, yep, even veggies got the treatment. It rated, as they say, roofwards. And no wonder.

So here, in your hands, is the most sensible thing for the Topps to have done next – a book from the series, so full of beautiful pictures it's almost like watching TV. And with stories from the Topps, recipes and timeless poetic musings from the (timeless) Kens, not to mention Camp Mother's Saucy Tips.

A grateful nation heads for the kitchen.

FOR THE LOVE OF
PORK

WE LOVE PIGS!

Some people might think that it's a contradiction that we love animals and also love eating meat – but we grew up on a farm so were born and raised to be meat-eaters. We choose to eat meat from animals that have had a happy life. Of course the best thing is to hunt your own meat – then you really appreciate where it has come from – but the next best thing is to support ethical farmers. Did you know that pigs are one of the most intelligent animals in the world, ranking close behind apes and dolphins? So it's very important that they are farmed ethically.

Jools and I passionately believe all pigs should be free-farmed and New Zealanders must demand an end to caged pork. If more consumers choose to buy free range then this cruel practice will end.

We've been around a lot of pigs and have learnt a lot about them, including that they are very clean – so the phrase "as dirty as a pig" is simply not true! They have a well-developed sense of smell and can be used to find truffles or sniff out drugs. Soldier pigs have even gone to war to sniff out mines on battlefields. In a natural environment they are capable of making friends and often have a circle of 20 "best mates". There are nearly one billion pigs in the world and pork is the world's most widely eaten meat – so farms such as Havoc Farm in Canterbury are a shining example of how to farm pigs with kindness – let's export this compassionate animal husbandry to the world!

LORD AND LADY HAVOC

Havoc Farm in Waimate is one of the happiest pig farms on the planet. Owners Ian and Linda Havoc are affectionately known as Lord and Lady Havoc. Scottish-born Ian grew up on a pig farm in England and had a lifetime of watching pigs being treated badly. His dream was to raise free-range pigs, so after travelling the world he finally found the perfect place to make his dream a reality – here in New Zealand in the foothills of South Canterbury.

He met the love of his life, Linda, at a local dance and they started an unlikely middle-age love affair. She was a city girl, who left her high-powered job as a human resources consultant behind, and has never been happier. Linda says she learnt patience when she came to the farm, because pigs do things in their own time.

The farm is well-named because havoc happens occasionally – like when the piglets get drunk on the ripe cherry plums or when Yuri the boar jumped the gates. Ian's policy has always been minimal intervention, no antibiotics, and no growth promoters – just a good old healthy diet of locally grown grain and a few added ingredients such as garlic and cider vinegar to keep the pigs happy and healthy. As Ian explains, "I would not feed my pigs anything I would not eat myself". We can attest to the fact that his farming methods certainly result in very tasty pork as we found out eating Nana's Bacon Balls (see page 18), a prized family recipe.

www.havocfarmpork.co.nz

NANA'S
⊱ BACON BALLS ⊰

SERVES 4-6 + PREP TIME 10 MINS + COOK TIME 25 MINS

INGREDIENTS

250g packet Havoc
   Bacon Mince or
   Minced Havoc Bacon
   Rashers or Pieces
1 cup grated cheese
1 cup rolled oats
1 large potato, peeled
   and grated
Pinch of cayenne
   pepper

METHOD

1 Preheat oven to 160°C.

2 Mix all ingredients together until well combined; you will
   need to do it with your hands. Form into balls about the
   size of a rounded teaspoon, or larger if you wish.

3 Place into an oven dish in rows (don't use an oven
   tray as the grease from the bacon and cheese will run all
   over your oven).

4 Bake until cooked (about 25 minutes).

5 Serve hot or cold.

"NO MAN SHOULD BE ALLOWED TO BE PRESIDENT WHO DOES NOT UNDERSTAND HOGS."
– FORMER US PRESIDENT HARRY TRUMAN –

GEOPRGE, MARINA,
MARY, MARIANO & MAIA
- A SPANISH / NEW
ZEALAND LOVE STORY

A SPANISH-NZ LOVE STORY

In 1985 Mary Davison left her home town of Christchurch and set off on her OE. Four years later she landed in Barcelona and joined a seven-piece female a cappella group called the Stupendams. After first hearing *Ngā Iwi E* sung by Jools & Lynda at Otago Uni when she was a student, Mary taught the group to sing the song in Māori, and they went on to record it on their first self-titled album. The vowel sounds in Spanish are the same as Māori so the Spanish picked up the song easily. It became a favourite part of the group's repertoire and it is now sung by many Catalan choirs.

Mary spent 17 years living in Barcelona working as a musician and actor with many different theatre and dance companies, and music groups, touring Europe. She fell in love with a (not-so) tall, dark and handsome Spaniard, Mariano Vivas, and before too long gave birth to two beautiful daughters, Marina and Maia.

In 2006 the family moved back to Christchurch to help take care of Mary's mum, Thelma. Yearning for the authentic flavours of home, and unable to find chorizo that tasted like the Spanish original, Mariano (with countless hours of perfecting) tweaked his age-old family recipes and 'Mariano's Spanish Goods' was born. His mother always said to him, "Whatever you do, you must do with love", and this has been his motto in the kitchen (and elsewhere!) ever since.

After Mary's mum passed away, her dad Gerald (George) moved in with them and the family became a tight-knit team as we discovered when we met them on the streets of Christchurch. Sadly George passed away in 2018, just short of his 90th birthday. He was quite a celebrity himself, as he invented the axial-flow jet unit enabling Bill Hamilton to commercialise his Hamilton Jet Boat. He worked for Hamiltons all his life and left quite a legacy in the jet boating world.

RIP George. You were a true gentleman of the old-school variety!

STIR FRIES • FILLET MIGNON

Organic
Mince

Mary, Mariano, Lynda & Jools sing Nga Iwi E outside Banfields Organic Butcher's shop

NGA IWI E

*(Sydney Hirini Melbourne,
Courtesy of Hirini Melbourne Whanau Trust)*

Ngā Iwi E
Ngā Iwi E
Kia kotahi ra
Te Moana nui-a-Kiwa x2
EIAIE EIAIE
Kia mau ra
Kia mau ra
Ki te mana motuhake
Me te aroha x2
EIAIE EIAIE
Wahine mā
Wahine mā
Maranga mai
Maranga mai
Kia Kaha x2
EIAIE EIAIE
Ngā Iwi E
Ngā Iwi E

Kia kotahi ra
Te Moana nui-a-Kiwa x2
EIAIE EIAIE
EIAIE EIAIE

TRANSLATION:
All the nations
All the nations
Let the people of the Pacific
Rim be united
EIAIE EIAIE
Listen and support it
EIAIE EIAIE
Hold on, Hold on
To your independence
and compassion
Women, Women
Rise up and be strong!

Ngā Iwi E was originally written for the fourth Festival of Pacific Arts in New Caledonia in 1985, and became the anthem song for the Nuclear Free and Independent Pacific movement.
We were with Hirini Melbourne when he composed it, and Mereana Pitman, Jools and I helped with cadences and some verses. We were all supposed to be going to the festival but decided to boycott it in solidarity with Kanak and Socialist National Liberation Front (FLNKS) as protest against French colonial rule.

• You can download the Topp Twins version from iTunes

MARIANO'S
CHORIZO OUS AL PLAT
(EGGS ON A PLATE)

SERVES 4 + PREP TIME 5 MINS + COOK TIME 20 MINS

INGREDIENTS

2 tbsp olive oil

250g fresh (not cooked) chorizo, roughly chopped

5 free-range eggs

½ cup milk

½ cup cream

Salt and black pepper, to taste

¼ cup roughly grated Manchego or Parmesan or similar cheese

Fresh parsley

METHOD

1 Preheat oven to180°C on the grill setting.

2 Add olive oil to a frying pan and fry the chorizo over a medium heat until it begins to brown (not more than 7 minutes). Set aside.

3 In a bowl, mix 1 egg with milk and cream and season with salt and black pepper. Add to the pan with the chorizo or transfer chorizo to an oven dish and add the egg mixture if your frying pan isn't ovenproof. Gently break in the remaining eggs and sprinkle cheese on top. Put frying pan/dish in oven for 5-6 minutes or more time if you prefer your eggs well-cooked.

4 Sprinkle the fresh parsley on the top and serve immediately with crusty bread. Enjoy!

IT WAS A BEAUTIFUL DAY AT ORTON BRADLEY PARK IN CHARTERIS BAY WITH ANNA, JOHN, ELIZABETH, EVIE & HUGH MAHY AND FRIENDS!

PIG IN A DAY WITH ANNA MAHY

John and Anna moved to New Zealand from Guernsey in the Channel Islands 13 years ago. Moving here sparked Anna's passion for making free-range charcuterie products after finding it difficult to find good-quality small goods here. For the last nine years they have been running Pig in a Day Workshops using pork sourced from Cressy Free Range Farm in Greendale, Canterbury. They've been teaching people how to make sausages, salami, chorizo, pancetta, bacon, ham and prosciutto.

Her main aim is to demystify and simplify the preparation of food using skills that used to be passed from generation to generation. She wants people to see how achievable it is, no matter what your skill level or size of kitchen.

Anna reckons that *"Food brings people together, friendships are forged, communities built and journeys shared around a table".*

Jools and I can testify that's true!

ANNA'S BRINE PORK ROAST

SERVES 4-6 + PREP TIME 15 MINS + CHILLING + BRINING + COOK TIME 2 HOURS

INGREDIENTS

The Brine
1 litre water
1 cup kosher salt (or plain non-iodised salt)
½ cup rich dark brown sugar or maple syrup
1 litre cider (get a good-quality traditional cider, avoid the sweetened ones)
2 tsp black peppercorns
3 tbsp coriander seeds
2 tbsp juniper berries
4 bay leaves

The Meat
2kg pork roast

METHOD

1 Place 500ml of the water in a saucepan with the salt and sugar (or syrup) and heat, stirring, until all is dissolved. Pour it into a 3 litre-capacity plastic box or non-reactive container and add the rest of the water plus the cider.

2 Toast the peppercorns and coriander in a dry saucepan, then grind them and add to the brine. Crush the juniper berries and add to the brine along with the bay leaves.

3 Chill - the brine must be cold before you put your meat in. Once it is well chilled place your pork in the brine and place a weight on top to keep it totally submerged. I find a side plate normally does the trick. Chill for 6 hours.

4 Take out, pat dry and let it sit at room temperature for an hour. Make sure the skin is dry. Score the skin into the fat (but not into the meat). Grind a little salt and pepper over the top.

5 Put it straight into a very hot 250°C oven. Check it after 15 mins. Once you see the skin starting to crackle you can turn it down to 170°C. It is ready when the internal temperature reaches 71°C (about 60 minutes per kg).

Check out www.preserved.co.nz for more of Anna's delicious recipes, as well as info on her workshops and café - Preserved Eatery in Diamond Harbour, Banks Peninsula.

KEN'S
❧ POEM ❧

WHEN I WAS A BOY,
I HAD A WEE PIG

I FED HIM LOTS
AND I TAUGHT HIM TO DIG

HE DUG UP THE GARDEN
AND HE ATE MY BEST SPUD

AND IN THE AFTERNOON
HE'D WALLOW IN MUD

I LOVED THAT SWINE,
I'M PARTIAL TO PORK

JESUS KEN, YOU'RE A FLAMING DORK!

HE WAS DESTINED FOR THE POT,
I LOVE A GOOD STEW

BUT HE LOOKED AT ME AND SAID
"KEN, I LOVE YOU"

I JUST COULDN'T DO IT,
I LET HIM RUN FREE

AND NOW ALL I EAT,
IS VEGGIES FOR TEA

FOR THE LOVE OF
SHEEP

BAAA-ME
⊰ ABOUT LAMB ⊱

There are about 40 million woolly critters grazing in Aotearoa right now, which is a sheep-load more than us Kiwis. New Zealand may be 'dairy country' now but our economy was founded on the export of lamb and mutton on the first refrigerated boats in the 1880s. 130-plus years on and NZ lamb is deemed to be the best in the world.

Lynda now lives in Staveley, Mid-Canterbury, and her neighbours Linda and Murray Harmer raise lamb fit for a queen. Murray reckons it's the quality of our grass and water, and the loving care the animals receive, that makes NZ lamb the tastiest in the world.

Farming large runs of sheep on a high country station in the South Island may look romantic but it's also a lot of work, as we found out when we joined Murray's brother Paul and his wife Kerry on their autumn muster at Castleridge Station.

Succulent lamb roast is not the only tasty thing a sheep can produce …not many people realise sheep can also be milked. We also learnt that sheep love yodelling – who knew!

Kiwis should be really proud of the produce we're turning out in this country and even prouder of the people who make it happen.

As Ken Moller would say – "They're *bloody gorgeous!*"

GETTING READY FOR THE MUSTER WITH KERRY HARMER AT CASTLERIDGE STATION

KEN'S
POEM

IT'S TIME AGAIN FOR MUSTERING
GET IN BEHIND THE SHEPHERDS SING
10,000 SHEEP COME DOWN
THAT HILL
GET OUT OF IT FLO
COME UP A BIT BILL

THEY WORK THAT MOB DOWN
TO THE SHED
GET OUT OF IT FLO!
GET AWAY BACK TED

THIS HIGH COUNTRY LIFE,
OH, IT IS FOR ME
OF MAN AND DOGS AND BILLY TEA
BUT HIGH ON A CLIFF THERE'S
A MIGHTY RAM
BUGGER! THE BOYS HAVE MISSED HIM
GET AWAY BACK SAM

GET OUT OF IT YA BLOODY MONGREL!
GET AWAY BACK YA BUGGER!
COME HERE, SLOW DOWN,
BRING 'EM IN
GOOD ON YA, BOY

THE HARMER FAMILY

Broken in by intrepid Scottish settlers, New Zealand's high country sheep farms were once the backbone of farming and the Kiwi economy. But these days only the brave farm sheep. It's a family affair here in Canterbury. Brothers Paul and Murray Harmer have sheep in their blood!

The meat Murray farms up at Winterslow Station is so good it's not sold in NZ and cannot be got here for love nor money. It all goes directly to the UK, where Murray is the poster 'boy' for Waitrose supermarkets. Rumour has it that the lamb that comes off this place ends up on a particular dinner table in England... Lizzie, mother of four... you know who that is don't ya?

Murray and his wife Linda also run a homestay in Staveley. Linda is an amazing cook and shared her delicious roast lamb recipe with us.

Kerry and Paul Harmer are passionate high country sheep farmers living the dream on Castleridge Station under the Southern Alps. It was a real privilege to help out on their muster. The dust, drama and taste of a high country muster of 20,000 sheep at Castleridge is an unforgettable experience. Let's face it, it's gotta be the most gorgeous office in the world!

KERRY'S ❧ ROSEMARY & ORANGE ❧ LAMB MARINADE

MAKES ENOUGH FOR ONE CUT OF LAMB + PREP TIME 10 MINS

INGREDIENTS

1 bunch of fresh rosemary, finely chopped

Zest and juice of 1-2 oranges

Ground black pepper, to taste

1-2 tbsp of good-quality olive oil

Salt, to taste

METHOD

1 Mix all ingredients, except salt, in a bowl and rub/massage well into the meat. Set aside for as long as you have, can be overnight. Add salt directly to meat just before putting meat on to cook.

KERRY'S TIP

● This marinade works for fillets/backstraps and chops - tender cuts are best. If using chops don't use shoulder chops as they are not tender enough and don't trim all the fat off, you need some for flavour and to keep the lamb moist.

LINDA'S ❧ OAT-CRUSTED ROAST ❧

SERVES 6 + PREP TIME 10 MINS + COOK TIME 1½-2½ HOURS

INGREDIENTS

½ cup rolled oats

2 tbsp bush honey

¼ cup olive oil

A good handful of mint, finely chopped

1 large leg of lamb

Salt, to taste

METHOD

1 Preheat oven to 150°C fanbake.

2 Combine all ingredients, except lamb and salt, in a bowl and let sit for a while.

3 Place lamb leg in a lidded oven dish, sprinkle with salt, then coat top with oat mixture.

4 Pour about an inch of water into the bottom of the oven dish - you don't want the lamb to dry out so you may need to add more water later. Cover and bake for 2½ hours, taking the lid off for the last 20 minutes. For a rare leg of lamb roast for 40 minutes per kilogram (1 hour 15 minutes for a rare 2kg roast). Remove and let sit, covered, while you make gravy from the juices. Enjoy.

THE GREAT NZ SHEEP RESCUE

For years as we have travelled around NZ, we have stopped to help out any sheep in strife that we see. We are up to number 158. While we were filming *Topp Country* we stopped to help out this poor old guy tangled in some blackberry. The only 'tool' we had was a pair of little fold-out nail scissors supplied out of the handbag of our production manager! While we tried to untangle him, she waved down some folk in a passing motorhome who, after being convinced we weren't some dodgy mass murderers, added a rusty stanley knife to the mix.

We got him free, carried him clear of the brambles and let him go. He bounced around like a young fella and shot off to his girls at the bottom of the paddock. In our jubilation and rush to get back on the road we managed to leave Lynda's suitcase behind, which we retrieved later that night after a bit of a search from the local police station only to discover we had actually backed over it! Ken Moller, who was in the suitcase at the time, was thankfully unharmed. Never a dull moment on the road!

KINGSMEADE SHEEP CHEESE

Miles and Janet King are award-winning artisan cheesemakers, and sheep breeders, with a positive and some might even say a "ewe-nique" attitude to life.

Miles loves sheep and worked for much of his life as a shepherd, but that all changed when he discovered he had a knack for making cheese. Since 1998 the Kings have quietly created a broad range of supreme hand-crafted ewe and cow's milk cheeses on their idyllic 30-acre farm on the outskirts of Masterton, in the Wairarapa. They have also selectively bred the very first NZ breed of milking sheep. The DairyMeade breed was recognised in 2016 by the New Zealand Sheepbreeders Association. Miles and Janet even have a substantial flock of black milking sheep that are known as the "Wool Blacks". (They say it's as close as they will ever get to the national team!)

All the Kingsmeade sheep are known individually to Miles, who milks them twice daily and he shared with us a few secrets about cheesemaking. Using the finest ingredients and having a gentle spirit are both essential. The Kingsmeade flock's ancestors originally hail from Swedish stock (maybe that's why these sheep love yodelling – who knew!) and are just as happy to be patted as they are being milked.

None of the sheep at Kingsmeade are destined for the table. Big, contented and full of personality – no need to round them up at milking time, they hear Miles' voice and come on their own.

Calm and quietly spoken, Miles is hands-on from the first steamy breath of the newborn lambs to the daily milking, cheesemaking, cutting and packaging. Each batch of cheese is handmade in the factory on the farm, right next to the family home. Just down the road in Lansdowne Janet runs the Kingsmeade shop, cheerfully selling cheese and despatching orders all across New Zealand.

www.kingsmeadecheese.co.nz

MILES & JANET WITH
THEIR FLOCK AND
ELLIE THE SHEEPDOG

JANET'S BLUE CHEESY ❧ MUSHROOMS ❧

SERVES 4 ✦ PREP TIME 10 MINS ✦ COOK TIME 20 MINS

INGREDIENTS

4 portobello
  mushrooms
Olive oil, for brushing
4 knobs of butter
150g packet Tinui Blue
  Cheese
Ground black pepper,
  to taste
1 handful of walnuts,
  chopped
1 handful of cherry
  tomatoes, halved
Balsamic vinegar, to
  drizzle
Flat-leaf parsley, to
  garnish
Lettuce leaves and
  crusty bread, to serve

METHOD

1 Preheat oven to 200°C and line an oven dish with baking paper or tinfoil.

2 Peel the mushrooms if desired, place gill-side up in the oven dish and brush with olive oil.

3 Place a knob of butter and a generous sprinkling or slice of Tinui Blue on each mushroom. Season with black pepper and bake for 20 minutes, or until mushrooms are soft.

4 Scatter over walnuts and cherry tomatoes, drizzle generously with balsamic vinegar and garnish with parsley. Serve on lettuce leaves with crusty bread on the side. Couldn't be easier!

HEALTH BENEFITS OF SHEEP CHEESE:

Not only do sheep milk products taste delicious but they also carry great health benefits such as being more acceptable to the human digestive system compared to cow's milk.
Sheep milk contains about one-third more energy than cow's or goat milk (making it a favourite of high-performance athletes). It has double the protein and much more of the right kinds of fats, vitamins and minerals, particularly calcium, iron, magnesium, phosphorus and zinc, while also being lower in sodium.

FOR THE LOVE OF
SALMON

ON THE FLY

Jools loves her horses but, for me, fly-fishing on New Zealand's rivers is about as close to heaven as I could get without actually being there. I have caught many beautiful brown and rainbow trout over the years (like the one above) but have never hooked up with a salmon. In New Zealand and Canadian rivers, both renowned for their big fiery fish, salmon have eluded my endless miles of walking the river's edge and even eluded me in the deep waters from a jet boat! I have made traditional Scottish salmon flies and given them to friends as presents and within 15 minutes of their first cast with those flies they've had tight lines, screaming reels and lovely big salmon – I, on the other hand, have had no luck at all! But, I have the consolation of knowing that my handmade flies do the job. I practise catch and release when fishing for trout and believe we need to support this in order to restock our rivers with good strong fish for the next generation. Our rivers must be treated with respect, everything must be done to keep them clean and healthy. I live only a few minutes from the beautiful Rakaia River, one of New Zealand's great salmon fisheries, so I guess I'll just have to keep trying. Until that day of my first hook up I will have to rely on the generosity of other great fishermen and fisherwomen for my next feed.

HIGH COUNTRY SALMON

Margaret Logan is the Jean Batten of the South Island's high country salmon farming. She is a very inspiring woman. Together with husband Richard, Margaret pioneered the very first (and only) fresh water salmon farm in the world, farming their Chinook salmon in Meridian Energy's glacier-fed waters of the hydro canals in the South Island's MacKenzie Basin.
The canals link mountain lakes and their swift, cold and pure waters produce a smaller fish with differing culinary attributes to their sea-reared cousins. Fresh water farmers use net pens anchored to the side of the canals and the strong flowing currents continually flush the farms, ensuring the water remains in pristine quality.
Margaret and her team work hard to give back to the surrounding community and all the donations for fish feeding are given back to local groups. They also run school visits in conjunction with the Department of Conservation, believing it is vital to educate our kids about sustainability.
Sadly, Richard passed away in 2012, leaving Margaret, the queen of Chinook farm salmon, to manage the entire operation with the help of the family's next generation.

www.highcountrysalmon.co.nz

MARGARET AND RICHARD LOGAN, FOUNDERS OF HIGH COUNTRY SALMON

DID YOU KNOW:

New Zealand is the only place in the world where Chinook salmon have been established successfully outside their native home of North America and North East Asia. They were introduced from eggs sourced from the McCloud River in California in the early 1900s. They were released into the Hakataramea River in the South Island and were soon running up other Canterbury rivers.
Chinook are a sacred tribal totem of the Winnemem Wintu people from California where the salmon were thought to have become extinct until links were discovered to Chinook salmon here.
A delegation have been working with local Maori iwi, Ngāi Tahu, and Fish & Game New Zealand over their plans to reintroduce the salmon to their native waterways back in California. Which won't be an easy task – only one percent of salmon eggs make it to full maturity.

JEREMY'S SALMON & SALSA ⇌ BURGERS ⇌

SERVES 4 + PREP TIME 10 MINS + BRINING + COOK TIME 10 MINS

INGREDIENTS

50g table salt
1 litre cold water
300g high country salmon
    fillet
Salt and ground black
    pepper, to taste

Avocado Salsa
100ml olive oil
Zest and juice of 1 lime
1 tsp toasted cumin seeds
A generous dash of mango
    hot sauce
1 chilli, seeds removed
    and finely diced
Flesh of 2-3 ripe avocados,
    diced
1 good handful of
    chopped coriander
Salt and ground black
    pepper, to taste

To Serve
Bread rolls, halved and
    toasted if desired
Aioli
Slices of tasty cheese
Baby rocket

METHOD

1 Place salt and water in a non-reactive bowl and whisk together. Add the salmon and set aside for about 30 minutes.

2 For the Avocado Salsa, combine all ingredients in a large bowl and set aside for at least 30 minutes to allow the flavours to infuse.

3 When ready to cook, preheat the barbecue hotplate to a high heat. Remove salmon from the brine and rinse under cold, fresh water before patting dry with a paper towel. Season both sides of the fish with salt and pepper.

4 Cook salmon until the flesh just flakes apart – be careful not to overcook it!

5 Assemble the burgers. Spread bread roll tops with aioli and place cheese slices on the bottoms. Flake salmon over the cheese and top this with Avocado Salsa – if you like you can smash up the salsa with a potato masher or fork first to make it more spreadable. Finish with some baby rocket and the bread roll tops. Serve while the salmon is still warm.

JEREMY'S TIP
● When cooking salmon on the barbecue, always give it a quick brine to ensure that it stays moist, despite the intense heat applied to the fillet on a hot plate.

BRUCE'S
COLD SMOKED
SALMON

INGREDIENTS

1kg salmon, filleted
Lemon pepper

The Brine

100g Honey Glo Cure or
   Rycol brine seasoning
100g sea salt
1 litre of hot water

To Serve

Crackers
Sour cream
Paprika

METHOD

1 Add Honey Glo Cure and salt to water in a large non-reactive container and stir to dissolve. Set aside to cool before using.

2 Place salmon fillets in brine, ensuring they are fully submerged. Leave in brine for 48 hours, turning every 12 hours.

3 Remove fillets from brine and rinse and drain thoroughly. Sprinkle with lemon pepper. Place in front of a cooling fan to thoroughly dry the salmon – approximately 12 hours.

4 Place in cold smoker for about 4 hours.

5 Remove, slice thinly onto crackers with a dob of sour cream and a sprinkle of paprika and enjoy.

BRUCE'S TIPS

- Cold smoking means the temperature of the smoke is less than 30°C.

- Brine seasonings are available at most butcher shops.

- You'll need eight coal shovels worth of fruit tree shavings for the smoker – I use 'Black Boy' peach tree shavings.

RAKAIA SALMON FISHING WITH BRUCE REILLY

Bruce has been fishing the Rakaia River since he was a boy. In fact he's a bit of a legend round these parts. He bottles and smokes his own salmon (both cold and hot).

When he's not fishing, he's also pretty skilled at pulling a pint – Bruce and his wife, Heather, had been running the Dunsandel Pub for 30 years when we first met him.

The pub runs a weigh-in competition during the season, attracting people from far and wide to see if they're going to be the next world record holder.

These days he has a lot more time to spend on the river, salmon is one of the hardest game fish to catch after all and good things take time!

RAKAIA GORGE, CANTERBURY

FRANK AND HILMA

We met mental health nurses Frank and Hilma salmon fishing in the hydro canals in the MacKenzie Basin. They told us they'd decided to put their own mental health first, so chucked in their day jobs and hit the road for six months in their rather flash caravan, living off the land, hunting and gathering wild food. They're both incredibly good at salmon fishing and since we had no luck we took up their offer of a good feed.

FRANK'S
✕ CRAB APPLE SALMON ✕
WITH KELP CHIPS

SERVES 4 ✢ PREP TIME 20 MINS ✢ COOK TIME 10 MINS

INGREDIENTS

Barbecue Wild Salmon
1kg salmon, filleted
4 tbsp crab apple or
  guava jelly

Kelp Chips
Fresh kelp (aim for
  smaller fronds about
  10cm wide)
Knob of butter
About 2 tbsp olive oil

Wild Salad
2 cups watercress
1 handful of mint,
  chopped
½ cup walnuts,
  chopped
2 pears, sliced
Flesh of 1 avocado,
  sliced
6 mandarins
Olive oil, to taste
Salt and ground black
  pepper, to taste

METHOD

1 Rub salmon with crab apple jelly and leave for a few minutes to go sticky.

2 Put into a hot barbecue with the skin side down, close the lid and cook for about 10 minutes. Take out and leave to set, with the crab apple jelly forming a lovely piquant glaze.

3 For the Kelp Chips, wash kelp in fresh water to get rid of any slime and grit.

4 Cut into strips about as wide as a little finger and fry in butter and olive oil mixture over a high heat until crispy. They turn a beautiful bright green before going brown and crispy when cooked. Beware that they can explode and fly around the place on occasions but this just adds to the experience!

5 To make the Wild Salad, toss together fresh watercress tips gathered from a clear stream with wild mint, roadside walnuts, pear and an avocado bought from a roadside stall.

6 Finish off by squeezing half a dozen mandarins and a drizzle of olive oil over it for the dressing. Season to taste with salt and pepper.

KEN'S POEM

I'VE ALWAYS BEEN A FISHERMAN
AND IT SETS MY HEART A QUIVER

TO SEE THE MIGHTY SALMON
RUN UP THE RAKAIA RIVER

THEY'RE BEAUTIFUL, THEY'RE ELUSIVE
THEY'RE A CHARMING WILD FISH

AND TO KEEP THE RIVERS CLEAN
AND CLEAR
WOULD BE MY HEARTFELT WISH

THERE'S NOTHING MORE EXCITING
THAN A TUG UPON YOUR LINE

IF YOU HAD IT YOUR WAY MATE
YOU'D BE FISHING ALL THE TIME!

TOO RIGHT! COLD SMOKE
AND EKETAHUNA WINE.

FOR THE LOVE OF
VENISON

DEER,
~ MY DEAR ~

When Jools was diagnosed with breast cancer I researched what foods she should eat and found out that venison is highly recommended as it's hormone-free, so I went out, shot a wild stag and stacked Jools' freezer with wild venison steaks. We've loved eating it ever since.

Venison is low in fat and has more protein than any other red meat. It is also particularly rich in iron and full of B vitamins, which may help to regulate metabolism and help protect against heart disease and cancer.

Large-scale commercial farming of deer actually started in New Zealand, and we now have the world's largest and most advanced deer-farming industry. The first deer were brought here from England and Scotland for sport in the 19th century and, after thriving here, quickly got out of control. Pioneers saw an opportunity and in the early 1970s started capturing live deer from the wild and farming them. A new industry was born.

We were lucky to experience the thrill of getting dangerously close to a herd of wild deer at Makapua Station with Colin and Marg Baynes, as well as meeting deer farmers Tim Aitken and Lucy Robertshawe in Hawke's Bay, whose love of deer farming and family is a total inspiration. We were also excited to learn how to make our own knives under the guidance of a man with an incredibly sharp sense of humour.

JOOLS AND LUCY SHARE THEIR LOVE OF HORSES AND A GOOD CUP OF TEA!

FARMED VENISON

When we met Tim Aitken and Lucy Robertshawe with their daughter Willa (who shares Lucy's love of horses) and son Jim, they were grazing their deer and bulls beneath 4225 native trees. As well as 7ha of beautiful native bush neatly fenced off and protected under a covenant with the Department of Conservation. Their commitment to ecologically sustainable farming has won them both local and international awards over the years with their top-quality venison being exported and sold in Marks & Spencer and Waitrose in the UK.

Tim's a self-taught deer farmer. He started out farming sheep, but has now been involved in the deer industry for many years and is a passionate (and talented) venison cook.

TIM'S BARBECUED BACKSTRAP WITH BRANDY SAUCE

SERVES 6 + PREP TIME 35 MINS + COOK TIME 3-5 MINS APPROX

INGREDIENTS

Infused Oil
¼-½ cup good-quality olive oil
1 lime, cut into quarters
A few peeled whole garlic cloves
Couple of rosemary sprigs

Venison
Firstlight Venison Backstrap
Flaky salt, to season

Sauce
Sour cream
Wholegrain mustard
Brandy

METHOD

1 To make the Infused Oil, place all ingredients in a small pot and heat oil over a low heat. Set aside for 30 minutes so the flavours can infuse.

2 Preheat barbecue grill (don't use the hotplate) to a high heat. Brush grill and venison backstrap with infused oil. Season venison with salt.

3 Place venison on the grill, brush again with the oil, brown on all sides then reduce heat to medium and close the lid of the barbecue (if you don't have a lid it should still cook ok). Cook for 1 minute each side per cm of thickness. Once cooked, set venison aside to rest for 3-5 minutes before carving.

4 To make the sauce, heat a frying pan on the barbecue, add some sour cream and mustard and stir together, then add brandy. Allow to bubble and thicken slightly, then serve with the venison.

TIM'S TIMING TIPS

How do you tell when meat is cooked to your liking? Do the touch test. When you touch the top of each finger on one hand with the top of your thumb, the firmness in the muscle at the bottom of your thumb will change depending on which finger you're touching. This firmness can be compared to the firmness of cooked meat.

Rare: This feels the same as when the thumb muscle is softest, which is when the thumb is touching the top of the index finger.
Medium rare: Thumb is touching the top of the middle finger.
Medium: Thumb is touching the top of the ring finger.
Well done: Thumb is touching the top of the little finger.

You can also check for doneness by making a small cut into meat when you think it's ready but don't cut too much as you don't want the juices to escape.

WILD VENISON

Colin and Marg Baynes have been farming for more than 25 years throughout the North Island and couldn't think of anything they would rather do. They love the land and especially Makapua, which is more than a home and a farm to them - it is a dream and a passion. Colin and Marg have created an inspiring life for themselves and their five children on this remote block. Makapua Station at the foothills of Te Urewera is home to them and their 20 working dogs.

Colin is a rugged Kiwi bloke and a passionate deer hunter who has turned his love of hunting into teaching people, especially teenagers, about the thrill and rigour of the hunt.

He's also passionate about preserving the native bush and this means keeping the numbers of wild deer low. Several times a year he rounds up wild deer on his farm, which end up as fancy wild venison on tables all over Europe.

The herd originated from the Windsor Park strain of red deer and actually happened by accident. Many years ago, a trailer load of deer rolled at the nearby Makapua Bridge and the escapees are the nucleus of the indigenous red deer herd on Makapua. Colin has consistently culled inferior stags to raise the quality of the trophy heads roaming the Makapua bush today.

The deer caught the night before have never had any contact with humans but with careful and practised handling Colin goes straight in to ear tag them. He is crazy! The wild deer are then sent out into the paddock to fatten up before they head off to Europe.

www.makapua.co.nz

MARG'S
⚜ RUMP CURRY ⚜
WITH NAAN BREAD

SERVES 4-6 ✦ PREP TIME 20 MINS ✦ COOK TIME 2½ HOURS

INGREDIENTS

Curry
2 tbsp cooking oil
2 tbsp green curry paste
2 large onions, chopped
2kg venison rump or
  shoulder meat,
  chopped into chunks
2 x 400g cans tomatoes
2 x 400g cans coconut
  milk

Naan Bread
175ml warm water
1 tsp caster sugar
1 tsp salt
1 tsp fast-acting dried
  yeast
2 tbsp sunflower oil
4 tbsp natural yoghurt
450g strong white bread
  flour

**Naan Bread
  Flavourings
  (optional)**
6 tbsp chopped fresh
  coriander
2 cloves garlic, crushed
1 red chilli, deseeded
  and chopped

METHOD

1 Heat a large camp oven or heavy-based pot over a high heat. Add oil and heat. Add green curry paste and heat, stirring. Add onions and cook for a few minutes until soft and translucent.

2 Add venison and stir until the venison has heated and is slightly browned but isn't cooked all the way through. Add tomatoes and coconut milk and bring to the boil. Remove from heat immediately once it boils.

3 Set aside to cool and then place in the fridge. The curry is best eaten at least a day after cooking.

4 To make the Naan Bread, place ingredients in breadmaker, in the order recommended by manual. Place on dough cycle and, 5 minutes before the end of the cycle, add coriander, garlic and chilli, if using.

5 At the end of the cycle, transfer dough to lightly floured work surface, knock back and knead lightly. Divide into 6-8 even-sized pieces. Using a lightly floured rolling pin, shape each piece into a teardrop shape, about 5mm thick. Place on lightly greased baking sheet and cover loosely. Leave to rise for about 30 minutes, until puffy and doubled in thickness.

6 Heat a heavy-based frying pan or barbecue hotplate over a medium heat and cook naan bread, in batches, for 2-3 minutes on each side until golden.

MARG'S TIPS

● The secret to cooking venison is to use a high heat and cook it for the minimum amount of time. Don't let it boil or simmer for hours as the meat will become stringy and tough.

● You can add veges to the curry if you like, green beans, kumara and pumpkin work well.

● Indian breads are best served warm. To reheat them, wrap in foil and warm in a hot oven for 5 minutes.

MARG IS MORE THAN A DAB HAND IN THE KITCHEN - SHE'S A DAB HAND IN THE SHEARING SHED TOO WITH A WORLD RECORD TO PROVE IT!

OUR FINISHED KNIVES - JOOLS WENT FOR BEAUTY AND I WENT FOR BEAST!

BARRYTOWN KNIFEMAKING

Steve Martin wasn't always a knife maker. Far from it. In fact his first passion was manufacturing women's lingerie! Barrytown is home to an eclectic mix of artists and craftspeople and it was here, on the wild west coast of the South Island, that Steve found the piece of metal that changed his life. He took it home, heated it up, bashed it into shape and Barrytown Knifemaking was born. With his wife, Robyn, they have helped hundreds of people from all around the world make knives that truly are a work of art.

Under his careful guidance and watchful eye we made our own knives (Jools' with a deer antler handle) and got a taste of his incredibly sharp sense of humour! And now Jools and I have our favourite knives to eat our steaks with.

www.barrytownknifemaking.com

KEN'S
⫸ POEM ⫷

FROM OUR NATIVE BUSH
TO THE SCOTTISH MOOR

THERE'S NO FINER BEAST
THAN A STAG IN ROAR

A MAGNIFICENT SIGHT
FOR A MAN TO SEE

FALLOW, RED OR WAPITI

I SAW HIM THERE IN THE
EVENING SKY

AND I RAISED THE GUN UP
TO MY EYE

(WHAT HAPPENED THEN KEN?)

JUST WAIT... A FLICKER THERE
A GENTLE DOE

I DROP MY GUN
AND SHOOT MY TOE!

FOR THE LOVE OF THE
GARDEN

HOME GARDEN

Lynda's neighbours, the Hesketh family, are committed vegetarians, gardeners and animal lovers. The family lives off the land in Mid Canterbury, farming 15 acres of fruit and veggies under the shadow of the Southern Alps, which provide a splendid backdrop for everyone – bullocks included! Youngest son Sunny is a super-keen gardener and an even keener cook. It's so good to meet a young person so into his veggies for a change!

Karen is everything you can imagine an earth mother should be and has an intriguing method of keeping the family fit with her exercycle-powered flour grinder! She grinds enough grain each week to make all her own bread.

It was a misty ol' morning the day we visited but the sun soon came out and showed us *Daisy Meadows* in all her glory!

SUNNY, KAREN,
MIGHTY, CHINTAMANI
AND FRASER HESKETH
AT DAISY MEADOWS
WITH JOOLS AND LYNDA

SUNNY'S
BEETROOT &
~ FENNEL SOUP ~

SERVES 6-8 + PREP TIME 15 MINS + COOK TIME 45 MINS

INGREDIENTS

Oil or ghee, for frying
1 tsp fennel seeds
3 beetroot, peeled and
  grated
1 tsp salt
2 litres water
1 potato, 1 kumara or ¼
  pumpkin, peeled and
  cubed (optional)
1 cup buckwheat groats
  or quinoa
Coconut cream or sour
  cream (optional)
Crusty bread, to serve
  (optional)

METHOD

1 Heat oil or ghee in a large heavy-based pot.
   Add fennel seeds and fry for 1 minute or
   until they become fragrant. Add beetroot,
   salt, water and potato, kumara or pumpkin
   (if using), bring to a boil and then simmer for
   25 minutes.

2 Add buckwheat groats or quinoa and cook
   until soft (about 20 minutes).

3 Just before serving stir through coconut
   cream or sour cream, if desired. Serve with
   crusty bread, if desired.

HELEN'S
FIG & GOATS' CHEESE TART

SERVES 4 + PREP TIME 10 MINS + COOK TIME 20 MINS + GRILLING

INGREDIENTS

375g block puff pastry
1 egg, lightly beaten
½ cup Te Mata Just
 Fig Jam
120g soft goats'
 cheese
1 tsp chopped
 rosemary leaves
Salt and ground black
 pepper, to taste
3-4 ripe figs, sliced or
 cut into wedges
1 tbsp honey
Green salad, to serve

METHOD

1 Preheat oven to 180°C. Line a baking tray with baking paper.

2 Roll out the pastry to an 18cm x 30cm rectangle. Place on baking sheet, brush the top with egg and prick all over with a fork. Bake for 10 minutes. Remove from oven, lay another tray on top and return to oven for 10 minutes. Remove and allow pastry to cool slightly. Switch oven to grill function on medium-high.

3 Spread jam over pastry base, crumble cheese over, sprinkle with rosemary and season with salt and pepper. Lay figs on top.

4 Place under grill for 2-3 minutes until cheese is lightly golden. Drizzle with honey. Serve with a green salad.

TE MATA FIGS

The Te Mata Figgery in Havelock North produces 24 varieties of figs and it's all thanks to Murray Douglas and his wife Helen Walker following their dream. Murray, the former CEO of Sydney's city council, and Helen, a clinical psychologist, chucked in their high-flying city jobs, jumped on a plane homeward bound and headed to the Hawke's Bay. Five years later and there's a lot of jiggery pokery in the figgery... With the plumpest juiciest and most delicious figs you'll ever eat!

www.tematafigs.co.nz

KELMARNA GARDENS

Deep in the heart of central Auckland is a city farm and organic community garden. Kelmarna Gardens is dedicated to building a healthy community and environment and promoting sustainable living. There's even an onsite kitchen where gardeners can cook up what they grow and lunchtime at Kelmarna Gardens is a collaborative effort based on whatever is in the garden. When we visited to film *Topp Country* and met the gorgeous Julie Hooper, the gardens were sub-leased to a mental health provider whose clients used the gardens for therapy. Now the Kelmarna Gardens Community Garden Trust is seeking community support to keep the gardens open and revitalise the space as an active garden at the heart of the community. It's a special place that's close to our hearts - many years ago Jools even had her caravan parked up there!

For more information or to become a Friend of Kelmarna visit www.kelmarnagardens.nz.

JULIE'S KELMARNA WAIATA FRITTATA

SERVES 6 ✦ PREP TIME 20 MINS ✦ COOK TIME 40 MINS

The amounts and ingredients are variable due to seasonality and because it doesn't really matter! (just what you've got basically).

INGREDIENTS

6 medium potatoes, halved

Oil or butter, for frying

3-4 cups chopped onion

4-6 handfuls leafy green veggies (e.g. silverbeet, kale, spinach), coarsely chopped

½ cup water

8 free-range eggs

½-1 cup milk

2 handfuls fresh herbs (e.g. thyme, sage, parsley, oregano, rocket, garlic chives), finely chopped

4 cups grated cheese, plus extra for topping

Salt and ground black pepper, to taste

4-6 small capsicum, sliced

METHOD

1 Place potatoes in a pot of water and cook for 15-20 minutes until parboiled.

2 Meanwhile, heat oil or butter in large frying pan. Add onion and cook gently over a low heat until soft.

3 Add leafy green veggies to the pan, then add water and cover with lid so the veggies can wilt and soften.

4 Place eggs in a bowl and beat lightly. Add milk, herbs, cheese and season with salt and pepper. Stir to combine and set aside.

5 Drain potatoes, rinse under cold water and drain again. Cut into 1cm-thick slices.

6 Preheat oven to 180°C. Grease the base and sides of a deep baking tin. Place a layer of potato slices in the tin then layer alternately with onion-veggie mix and capsicum to just below the rim of the tin. Pour over egg mixture and sprinkle extra cheese on top, if desired. Bake for about 40 minutes. It is cooked when knife comes out clean from centre.

JULIE'S TIPS

• This is a flexi frittata - you can vary the amounts and ingredients depending on seasonality and what you have.

• For example instead of the potato you can use pumpkin; instead of onion you can use leek, spring onion, garlic, garlic chives or a combo of anything from the onion family; instead of capsicum use peeled and grated carrot, diced tomato or any colourful veggies.

KEN'S
~ POEM ~

THERE ARE SOME OF US THAT
DON'T EAT MEAT

THEY SAY YOU CANNOT BEAT
A BEET

LENTILS, MUNGBEANS,
VEGGIE STEW

CARROT JUICE AND
CREAMED TOFU

CASHEWS, ALMONDS,
NO IFS OR BUTS

ALL GOOD VEGOS
EAT THEIR NUTS

SO COME ON FOLKS
GIVE MEAT THE BOOT

AND GET YOURSELF
A HEALTHY ROOT!

"GET YOUR LINES OUT BOYS!"
THE CAPTAIN YELLS
ABOVE THE RAGING SEA THAT SWELLS

A GREAT RED SNAPPER
A SOFT BLUE COD
ALL CAUGHT WITH JUST A SIMPLE ROD

SO PRECIOUS IS THE LIFE WITHIN
TO FISH HER OUT
WOULD BE A SIN

AH, THE SEA, THE DEEP BLUE SEA
IT'S OURS TO SAVE
IT'S OUR LEGACY

– KEN MOLLER –

FOR THE LOVE OF
THE SEA

KAI MOANA

Although we may be identical twins,
there's one big difference between us – I love eating
all kinds of seafood, while poor Jools is allergic
to shellfish. One tiny trace of it and she has a massive
and instant reaction! So when we set off on a kai
moana gathering and cooking adventure, we had to
be very careful.

First stop is visiting our dear friend Fleur Sullivan. Fleur
is one of NZ's greatest restaurateurs – people travel
from all over the world to eat at the famous Fleur's
Place in Moeraki, in the heart of Otago. When British
television chef and restaurateur Rick Stein was told he
could choose to go anywhere in the world to write
a travel article for English newspaper the *Daily Mail*,
he chose Fleur's Place.

Jools and I have had the pleasure of knowing Fleur for
30 years and it's always a joy to see her again. Cooking
fish in kelp bags is an old Māori tradition and Fleur
adds her own gourmet twist to steaming blue cod.

FLEUR'S
⚜ COD & COCKLES ⚜
IN A KELP BAG

SERVES 2 + COOK TIME 20 MINUTES

INGREDIENTS

1 whole blue cod, cleaned
1 lemon, sliced
Fennel fronds (wild fennel grows in most of our coastal areas)
Fresh herbs (e.g. parsley)
Dark green bull kelp, cut from the thick end
A dozen cockles

METHOD

1 Catch your fish (in this case blue cod), gather your shellfish and source your bull kelp (this can be more difficult in the north than the south).

2 Scale, gill and gut your fish and put some lemon slices, fennel fronds and parsley in the gut cavity.

3 Prepare your kelp bag. Cut your kelp to suit the size of your fish and quantity of shellfish (30-45cm). Wash it well, making sure it's free from grit and sand. Cut through the kelp horizontally and form a pocket with your knife (think of it as a large pita pocket), making sure you do not puncture the kelp. I hold the kelp flat on the bench with one hand, forming the cavity with the other.

4 Place your prepared blue cod in north to south as if it had just swum in there. Place the cockles or other shellfish either side of the cod and fasten the kelp bag with a kebab skewer or with a harakeke (flax) thread, threading it through holes made by a kebab skewer. Place in a roasting dish.

5 Roast in a hot oven (about 180°C) for about 20 minutes until bloated from the internal steam and the shellfish open inside.

6 Serve at the table in the kelp bag. Carefully cut the kelp bag open by making a large cross cut in the centre and fold the four corners back to expose your fish and shellfish.

FLEUR'S TIPS

● Always ensure your kelp and shellfish are collected from pristine coastal waters.

● Choose kelp that is thick and spongy to touch - what you don't use can be dug into your garden.

HOTUROA KERR HAS BEEN SAILING WAKA FOR 20 YEARS AND TRAINING YOUNG MAORI IN THE SEAFARING WAYS OF OLD.

WAKA

We were lucky to sail the Hauraki Gulf on a magnificent waka, the *Haunui Te Waka Houra,* with John Panoho and his crew. This waka had recently returned from sailing around the world on a mission to raise awareness of the plight of the world's oceans.

Auckland City's Waitemata Harbour was discovered by waka-sailing Māori more than 800 years ago. They navigated their way here using only the stars, the sun and the wind. Imagine how they felt sailing into this harbour way back then. The ocean must have been literally leaping with life.

John's vision is to give everyone a waka-sailing opportunity and he's as passionate about our oceans as he is about cooking its bounty.

Recreational fishing and collecting seafood is an ingrained part of our culture, and with the Waitemata Harbour a shared backyard to our biggest city, there's nothing better than getting out on it and gathering a feed of fresh kai moana with friends and family. The Waitemata Harbour and Hauraki Gulf are a precious taonga and we must protect it for future generations so it can be enjoyed as we enjoy it forever!

www.navigatortours.co.nz

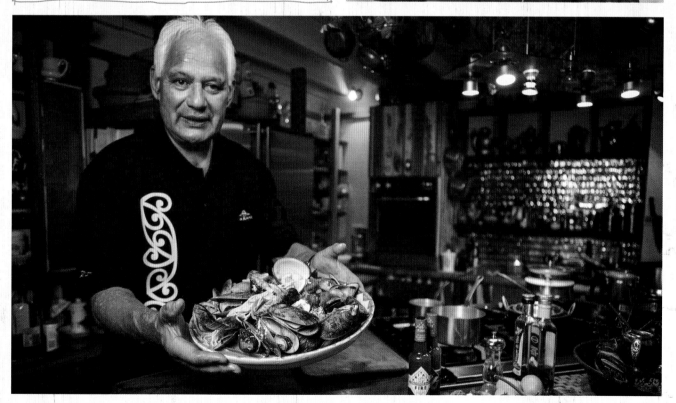

HAURAKI GULF, AUCKLAND

JOHN'S
MASHPEE INDIAN
⊱ CLAMBAKE ⊰

SERVES AS MANY AS YOU NEED TO FEED (ADJUST INGREDIENT QUANTITIES AS NECESSARY)
PREP TIME 20 MINS + COOK TIME 2 HOURS

This is best prepared in an earth oven, but we used a portable hangi cooker with manuka smoking dust. You could also use a steamer or slow cooker.

INGREDIENTS

Seaweed, cleaned
Red potato or kumara, scrubbed (leave skin on)
Corn on the cob
Smoked sausage, cut into chunks, or bacon bones
Pineapple, peeled, cored and sliced
Prawns
Clams (cockles or pipi), cleaned
Mussels, cleaned and debearded
Butter
Lime and/or lemon juice

To Serve
Melted butter
Lemon wedges
Coconut cream

METHOD

1   In baskets, lay down a first layer of seaweed and then alternate layers of food (except seafood) and seaweed, ending with a layer of seaweed. Place slower-cooking foods such as potatoes, corn, and kumara in the lowest layers with the sausage in the middle and reserve the seafood to put in the topmost layer later.

2   Place container of manuka chips in the base of the cooker and smoke baskets of food with the lid on for 20 minutes. Remove container of chips, replace food baskets and put water into cooker to create steam. Cook for a further hour and then add seafood on top layer with chunks of butter on top to melt through together with lemon juice, lime juice and/or water to continue steaming process. When the shellfish are open and slowest-cooking vegetables are cooked remove baskets (about 20-30 minutes).

3   Serve by dumping everything out onto newspaper, accompany with melted butter and lemon wedges and eat with your fingers. You can also strain the liquid from the cooker into a pot, bring it to the boil, add coconut cream and serve in a dipping bowl for prawns and mussels.

TERRAZA SAFFRON

Tasting saffron, they say, is like tasting sunshine on your tongue. The health benefits of saffron are many too - medical research suggests saffron can protect against cancer; in Japan it is used in the treatment of Parkinson's disease, memory loss and inflammation; it can help bring on menstruation and increase vitality and libido; it is also an effective remedy for colds and fever.

So it's no wonder saffron is one of the most sought after - and expensive - spices on earth. Derived from the flower of *Crocus sativus*, commonly known as the "saffron crocus", the vivid crimson threads are painstakingly collected and dried as a flavouring and natural colouring agent for food. Saffron has been traded and used for 4000 years. Iran accounts for 90 per cent of the world's supply, but now an enterprising Kiwi family is growing some of the world's finest saffron.

Terraza Saffron on the terraces of the Ngaruroro River valley, Hawke's Bay, is truly a family business. Mark Tyro, Janice Potts and their three young kids, Alex, Mackenzie and Cole, all harvest this beautiful flower in April - and it's very labour-intensive as Jools found out! As we know there is no better match for seafood than saffron so we asked Janice to share her signature dish.

www.terrazasaffron.co.nz

JOOLS GETTING MUSICAL WITH ALEX, MACKENZIE & COLE WHILE LYNDA & JANICE COOK UP A SEAFOOD FEAST

JANICE'S
SEAFOOD &
❧ SAFFRON PAELLA ❧

SERVES 4-6 ✦ PREP TIME 10 MINS ✦ COOK TIME 30 MINS

The beauty of this recipe is that you can add/remove seafood as your personal taste and fridge contents allows. So treat the recipe as a starting point and enjoy!

INGREDIENTS

8-10 NZ grown saffron threads (use more if you're using imported saffron)
Olive oil, for cooking
2 cloves garlic
1 onion, chopped
1 chorizo sausage, chopped (optional)
1 tsp smoked paprika
2 cups short-grain rice (e.g. Calasparra)
4 cups chicken stock
1 bay leaf
4-6 fish fillets (1 per person), cut into chunks
12-18 mussels (3 per person), cleaned and debearded
12-18 prawns (3 per person), deshelled

METHOD

1 Crush saffron threads in the palm of your hand, place in a small bowl, add 1 teaspoon warm/hot water and set aside to infuse for 10-20 minutes.

2 Meanwhile, heat oil in a frying pan over a medium heat. Add onion, garlic and chorizo, if using, and cook for a few minutes until onion is soft. Add paprika and continue to stir for 2 minutes.

3 Heat a little more oil in a paella pan, or a large flat frying pan. Add rice, stir to coat in the oil and toast over a medium heat until it starts to colour.

4 Add onion mix to rice in paella pan. Add chicken stock, bay leaf and the saffron infusion. Stir everything together and bring to the boil, stirring occasionally to ensure all the ingredients are distributed evenly.

5 Add pieces of fish and leave to simmer for 15 minutes. Do not stir, but turn the pan occasionally to ensure everything is cooked evenly.

6 Add mussels and prawns and cook until mussels open, all liquid has been absorbed and the rice is soft.

7 Turn off the heat and remove and discard bay leaf. Cover pan with a clean tea towel and leave to rest for 5 minutes. Serve warm from the pan.

FOR THE LOVE OF
BEEF

HOLY COW

Lynda and I grew up on a dairy farm and apart from a few obligatory years as vegetarians when we were younger, we have always loved our steak.
As good ol' country girls we've had our fair share of mince on toast, Sunday roast, corned beef and eye fillet steak. All cooked with love by our beautiful Mum from own our cattle raised on the farm by Dad.

It's how we were brought up, so Lynda and I have carried on that family tradition on our own lifestyle blocks. It's a big responsibility to care for these animals and give them the best stress-free life they can have. Two years of managing their grass intake, health care and trudging out in the cold winter to feed them a big pile of hay every day is part and parcel of growing your own healthy food.

Home-raised and home-killed beef means the animal has a much less stressful death and the meat not only tastes better but it's better for you. If you're going to eat meat then consider where it comes from and try to eat more consciously.

KEN'S
POEM

COWS ARE MATRIARCHAL
AND AS FEMINIST AS CAN BE
NOW I'VE STUDIED THIS AT LENGTH
AND I THINK THE FACTS I'VE GOT
HAVE A LOT OF STRENGTH

FOR A START COWS LIVE TOGETHER
THEIR COMMUNAL SPIRITS HIGH
AND WHEN THEY SLEEP AND
EAT TOGETHER
IT BRINGS A MAN TEAR TO MY EYE

NOW DOG'S A MAN'S BEST FRIEND
SO SAYS THE SPECIES MAN
BUT A COW CAN'T BE A MAN'S
BEST FRIEND
'CAUSE SHE'LL KICK HIM IF SHE CAN

AND ALL THE TIME I'VE KNOWN COWS
AS SURE AS SHEEP HAVE WOOL
I'VE NEVER MEET A COW THAT JUMPED
THE FENCE TO SEE THE BULL

PIGEON BAY, BANKS PENINSULA

ANGUS BEEF

Our search for the country's most delicious beef brings us to one of the most spectacular places on the planet – Pigeon Bay on the Banks Peninsula where David and Belinda Hay farm Angus beef on their 500 hectare property. David took over Glenralloch when he was only 22 years old, and although it was a huge undertaking for someone so young, he's never regretted it. The farm is one of the oldest in New Zealand – it has been in his family for 174 years – and he and Belinda feel privileged to live in the family homestead. This farmer, like all we met on our journey around New Zealand, loves and nurtures his animals. David thinks cattle are very responsive animals – they're fascinated by humans and respond to the human voice, to changes in pitch and tone. David sure knows his beef and Belinda's roast Angus steak with smoked garlic was perfection itself, all washed down by a boutique beer made by James, one of the Hays' handsome sons. Heaven!

BELINDA'S
⚜ ROAST ANGUS ⚜
WITH SMOKED GARLIC

SERVES 6 + PREP TIME 5 MINS + COOK TIME 20-25 MINS PER KG

INGREDIENTS

Whole sirloin steak
    (about 2kg)
Olive oil, for cooking
Smoked garlic (see tip)
Rock salt

METHOD

1 Preheat barbecue to about 300°C (the temperature needs to be constant before putting the beef in).

2 Dry steak with paper towels. Rub all over with some olive oil and then rub in smoked garlic and rock salt. Place steak on a rack in a roasting dish.

3 Place the dish in the middle of barbecue. I have the outside two gas burners on, with the two middle gas burners turned off. Cook for 20 minutes per kg for rare, 25 minutes per kg for medium. Don't cook it any longer for 3kg as the depth of the steak is usually the same. Don't open the lid unless your barbecue retains the heat.

4 Rest for 15-20 minutes covered with tinfoil and a towel or tea towels to keep it warm. Carve and serve.

BELINDA'S TIPS

● To cook it in the oven, cook for 15 minutes at 200°C then at 15-20 minutes per kg at 185°C – I check it often as it does depend on the oven.

● To smoke garlic, rub a head of garlic with olive oil and smoke for 20 minutes.

JASON'S
BUTCHER'S PIE

SERVES 6 ✦ PREP TIME 1 HR ✦ COOK TIME 45 MINS

Makes one big pie or muffin tin-sized pies. Great to freeze for a rainy day! Make the filling the day before you make the pie.

INGREDIENTS

Olive oil, for cooking
4 onions, diced
2kg good-quality beef mince
4 carrots, peeled and grated
2 cups beef stock
1-3 cups water (enough to cover the meat in the pot)
2 heaped tbsp tomato paste
450g can tomato purée
Salt and ground black pepper, to taste
¼ cup cornflour, mixed to a paste with water to thicken
2x 750g packet flaky pastry sheets
2 cups grated tasty cheese
1 egg, beaten

METHOD

1 Heat some olive oil in a deep pan over a medium heat. Add onions and sauté for a few minutes until soft. Remove onions from pan and set aside.

2 Increase heat, add mince to the pan and brown the mince. When mince is browned, add carrots, reserved onions and beef stock and stir to combine. Add enough water to cover the meat by 2½cm, then add tomato paste and tomato purée. Cook, stirring often, for 30-40 minutes. Season to taste. Add cornflour mixture and stir through to thicken with sauce. Leave to cool overnight.

3 Preheat oven to 210°C. Use flaky pastry to line one big pie dish or cut into circles 4cm bigger than the size of each muffin tin and press into muffin tins to line. Fill with cold mince mixture to three-quarters full. Top with tasty cheese - as much as you like. Brush egg around the inside pastry edge, place a pastry lid on and press the edges together. Use a fork to press down the edges to seal and trim off any excess pastry. Use a fork to poke a couple of holes in the top to let steam escape. Brush the top with more beaten egg. Turn the oven down to 200°C and fanbake for 30-35 minutes for muffin-sized pies or 40-50 minutes for one big. Enjoy!

TIP

• If you freeze your pies, make sure to fully defrost them before reheating in a 150°C oven for 20 minutes.

THE BUTCHER'S PIES

For high-school sweethearts Jarnia and Jason Kupe, opening the Hororata Village Café and Bar at the foothills of the Southern Alps meant creating something that could finally be their own. Passionate about food and people, the café brought all their dreams together. As if running a busy café, and caring for their family isn't enough, these two loved-up people are also active volunteers in their community. Jarnia is a volunteer fire-fighter and Jason coaches the local rugby team. A butcher by trade, Jason started to bake the pies for the café, hence the name "The Butcher's Pie". From 200 pies a week to now well over 1000 pies a week, their pies have helped put Hororata on the map as a must-visit destination.

The most popular Butcher's Pie flavour? Definitely The Butcher's Steak & Cheese - the fussiest of fussy attention, lots of braising and love makes these pies worth a drive out to the country ! Hororata is just down the road from Lynda's place, so needless to say she's become a regular customer.

ET LUCKY

¡¡TACOS!!

PULLED PORK

VEGE

SPICY FISH

"TOPP" STEAK TACO!

CHIPOTLE PRAWN
$7 OR 2 FOR $12

LUCKY TACO

The Lucky Taco food truck is the love child of Otis and Sarah Frizzell and was conceived on their honeymoon in Las Vegas back in 2011. Turned on by each other and the flavour of street food culture, the ex-advertising copywriter and her artist hubby are now proud full time parents of an expanding "lucky" Mexican food empire.

The kitchen is not just the heart of the home for Sarah and Otis, it's the heart of their business. It's around the kitchen table that this couple of "enthusiastic home cooks" hatched the plan for their first enterprise, the Lucky Taco food truck. Otis and Sarah headed to Mexico City to learn authentic Mexican cooking. After spending six weeks driving around Mexico in a tiny red Fiat, and eating nothing but tacos – the most unusual being 'machitos' (sheep scrotum) – they came home and started cooking nothing but tacos. The Lucky Taco food truck was born, and quickly became a popular attraction, parked up on Ponsonby Road, or catering at private functions and festivals. We love Mexican and have enjoyed delicious authentic tacos in LA but their Taco de Arrachera (beef taco) is a sensation. If you want to try some of the Frizzell tasty magic, look for their taco kits, award-winning Pink Pickle, hot sauces and chilli salt online or at select food stores.

www.theluckytaco.co.nz

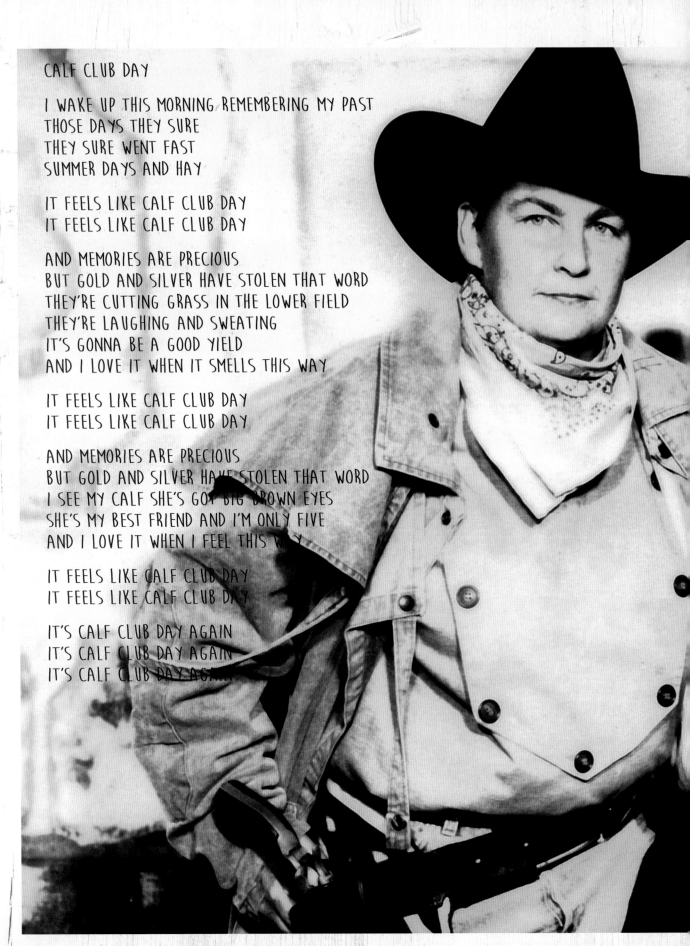

CALF CLUB DAY

I WAKE UP THIS MORNING REMEMBERING MY PAST
THOSE DAYS THEY SURE
THEY SURE WENT FAST
SUMMER DAYS AND HAY

IT FEELS LIKE CALF CLUB DAY
IT FEELS LIKE CALF CLUB DAY

AND MEMORIES ARE PRECIOUS
BUT GOLD AND SILVER HAVE STOLEN THAT WORD
THEY'RE CUTTING GRASS IN THE LOWER FIELD
THEY'RE LAUGHING AND SWEATING
IT'S GONNA BE A GOOD YIELD
AND I LOVE IT WHEN IT SMELLS THIS WAY

IT FEELS LIKE CALF CLUB DAY
IT FEELS LIKE CALF CLUB DAY

AND MEMORIES ARE PRECIOUS
BUT GOLD AND SILVER HAVE STOLEN THAT WORD
I SEE MY CALF SHE'S GOT BIG BROWN EYES
SHE'S MY BEST FRIEND AND I'M ONLY FIVE
AND I LOVE IT WHEN I FEEL THIS WAY

IT FEELS LIKE CALF CLUB DAY
IT FEELS LIKE CALF CLUB DAY

IT'S CALF CLUB DAY AGAIN
IT'S CALF CLUB DAY AGAIN
IT'S CALF CLUB DAY AGAIN

HOLY COW

TWO STEPS BACK, ONE STEP RIGHT
SWING HER ROUND AND HOLD HER TIGHT
DOSEY DOE AND TAKE A BOW
CIRCLE ROUND THE HOLY COW

MY GIRL LOVES TO SLIDE ON THROUGH
WHEEL HER ROUND AND SHOE FLY SHOE
HITCH THE HORSE UP TO THE PLOUGH
ALL SWING LEFT NOW HOLY COW

CENTRE IN AND ALL SCOOT BACK
SHOT THE STAR BY THE OLD TIN SHACK
THE BULLS JUMPED OUT,
I DON'T KNOW HOW
I THINK HE DID THE HOLY COW

YODEL

FOR THE LOVE OF THE
POULTRY

BIRDS OF A ❧ FEATHER ❧

Ever since I was little, I can remember Mum sending us off to feed the chickens and collect the eggs. It just felt like the most exciting thing to open the lid on the nesting boxes and see how many eggs the chickens had laid. So just like horses they have been a big part of our lives and I still get excited about putting on my gumboots and heading off with the billy to put the eggs in.

I once had a real pet hen who would come into the house every morning and sit on the floor and have bread while I had my morning cuppa then happily head off out the door to scratch around the farm. Auntie Ethel had a chicken that walked up the stairs to the house, marched down the hallway and laid an egg in a drawer of her tallboy every morning at 11 o'clock on the dot.

It will be a great day when the cruel practice of keeping birds caged in cramped conditions with no ability to walk in the sun and scratch in the dirt is stopped. It's quite easy to have chickens of your own if you have a good hen house and a commitment to care for them every day. They are fun little animals for kids to care for and the eggs are a great source of protein. You may have to fence off your vegetable garden or have them in a big run because they will certainly eat stuff you plant. Or failing that buy only free-range eggs at the supermarket, they may cost a little more but think of the happy hens who can flap their wings, pull a worm from the soil with a beak that hasn't been cut, shuffle around in a dust bath and have the freedom to roam while they work hard every day for us delivering beautiful eggs.

JOOLS, PHIL, LYNDA & JUDITH ROUND UP A 'RAFTER' OF TURKEYS

THE CROZIERS

For over 50 years, Judith and Phil Crozier have farmed free-range turkeys on their farm near Ashburton and built a wonderful reputation for using only organic processes, non-intensive farming methods and putting animal welfare first. Once the birds are fully feathered at 4-6 weeks, they roam freely enjoying a true free-range lifestyle, eating bugs and grasses, and communal dirt baths. The Croziers even make their own feed, grinding grain on the farm, and instead of adding antibiotics they use probiotics and blended essential oils. No wonder their turkeys taste so good! We were lucky to meet the Crozier family and their flock, just before they passed their legacy on to another NZ family with a passion for breeding truly free-range turkeys. Who knew a group of turkeys is called a "rafter"?

PHIL'S MUM'S
STUFFED TURKEY

SERVES 6 + PREP TIME 30 MINS + COOK TIME 2½ HOURS

INGREDIENTS

½ loaf bread
1 egg
1 onion, chopped
1 apple, peeled and
    chopped
2 tbsp orange juice
Mixed herbs, to taste
2 tbsp melted butter
Handfuls of parsley,
    chopped
Salt and ground black
    pepper, to taste
1 tsp baking powder
4-5kg turkey, washed
1 tube sausage meat
1 cup water

Baste

2 tbsp gelatin, softened
    in a little water
2 tbsp brown sugar
2 tbsp honey

METHOD

1 Preheat oven to 150°C. Sprinkle a little flour, salt and pepper in the bottom of a roasting dish and set aside.

2 Place bread in a food processor and pulse to form breadcrumbs. Place in a large bowl. Place egg, onion, apple and orange juice in the food processor and blend together. Add to the breadcrumbs and stir through. Add mixed herbs, melted butter, parsley (lots) and mix well. Season to taste with salt and pepper and stir through baking powder.

3 Place stuffing in large turkey cavity, without packing it in too tightly, and stuff the neck cavity with sausage meat. Place the prepared turkey in the prepared roasting dish, pour water around the turkey, cover with tinfoil and cook for the time indicated on the bag, about 20 minutes plus 30 minutes per kg. A cooking timer inserted in the turkey will indicate when it's cooked and check to see the juices run clear.

4 While the turkey is cooking, make the baste by mixing all the ingredients in a bowl with a little hot water to make a paste.

5 At the end of cooking, take the turkey out of the pan and drain most of the juices, then return to pan. Use a fork to stab the turkey all over, drizzle over the baste, scoop up from the bottom of the pan and spoon over again. Bake in the oven for another 10 minutes. Take out of oven, spoon baste over again and allow to stand before carving. You can also use the juices left in the pan to make a lovely, yummy gravy.

BENEFITS OF EATING TURKEY

Who knew turkey is so good for you! It is high in protein and low in calories, so can aid weight loss. It promotes better sleep as it's high in tryptophan, an amino acid that helps regulate sleep and even combat depression. Plus it is packed with selenium, which increases immunity, has been shown to have anticancer properties and decreases heart disease. So don't wait till Christmas to enjoy turkey!

ANNIE GUINNESS

Annie Guinness is an acclaimed chef from
Matakana, an hour north of Auckland, and is one
of the sibling founders of the well-known Leigh
Sawmill. Together with husband Phil and their three
kids, they swapped gumboots for jandals and took
over Auckland's iconic inner-city café Verona on the
infamous Karangahape or "K" Road. You can take
the girl out of the country but you can't take the
country out of the girl! The day we visited, Annie
was tending her herb garden on her roof-top
apartment, and she was getting ready to cook us
her mouth-watering delicious duck curry, which
people have queued up to buy at the Matakana
Markets. But first stop was a visit to Tony Chan at
Chinese Cuisine in Mercury Plaza. Annie reckons it's
the best Peking duck in Auckland. We promise that
this recipe will become a family favourite.

ANNIE'S DUCK CURRY

SERVES 6 + PREP TIME 20 MINS + COOK TIME 1½ HOURS

INGREDIENTS

Duck Curry

3 tbsp butter

1 cup diced fresh pineapple

2 tbsp sesame oil

1 tbsp black mustard seeds

2cm piece ginger, thinly sliced

1 clove garlic, thinly sliced

1 hot chilli, finely chopped

1 cup diced red capsicum

1 cup diced green capsicum

½ cup diced celery

1 tsp tom yum paste

1 cup brown lentils

Meat from 1 roasted Peking duck

Salt and ground black pepper, to taste

Duck Stock

1 roasted Peking duck carcass

2 kaffir lime leaves

2 star anise

2 tbsp soy sauce

1 tbsp brown sugar

To Serve

Rice

Coriander

METHOD

1 To make Duck Stock, place all ingredients in a pot, cover with water and simmer for at least a couple of hours. Strain and reserve stock, you will need about 1 litre.

2 Heat butter in a frying pan until nut brown. Add pineapple to pan and sauté until caramelised. Set aside.

3 Heat sesame oil in a pot. Add mustard seeds and cook until they start to pop. Add ginger, garlic and chilli and cook for 1 minute, then add capsicum, celery, tom yum paste, reserved pineapple and lentils. Stir well. Add reserved duck stock, cover pot and cook over a gentle heat for about 20 minutes until lentils are tender.

4 Add duck meat and adjust seasoning with salt and pepper. Serve on rice garnished with coriander.

A RARE BREED

Jools and I love chooks. Collecting fresh eggs in the morning is one of life's wee pleasures and clucking hens can only make you smile.
We met a woman who loves her chooks so much she spends more time on their hairdos than she does on her own! Raewyn Norton has a stunning flock of over 25 breeds of rare chickens on the heritage farm she runs with hubby Gary in the Waitakere Ranges – if you love birds and vintage machines this is the place for you! Who knew there were so many varieties? This place is teaming with lovely looking birds...

LYNDA GETS FRIENDLY WITH THE LOCALS AND GARY & RAEWYN NORTON SHARE SOME OF THEIR TREASURES

KEN'S
❧ POEM ❧

I LOVE BIRDS – I CANNOT LIE

BUT NOT THE TYPE THAT SOAR
ON HIGH

NOT THE EAGLE, OR THE
CHEERFUL WREN

YOU SEE, I'M DRAWN TO THE
COMMON HEN

JUST SIMPLE GRAIN AND SOME
GARDEN WEEDS

AND KITCHEN SCRAPS WILL MEET
HER NEEDS

THIS GOOD HEN HAS SERVED
US WELL

AND THIS GOOD STORY I MUST TELL

AT SUNRISE I WILL TEND MY FLOCK

AND ADMIRE MY GREAT
SPECKLED COCK

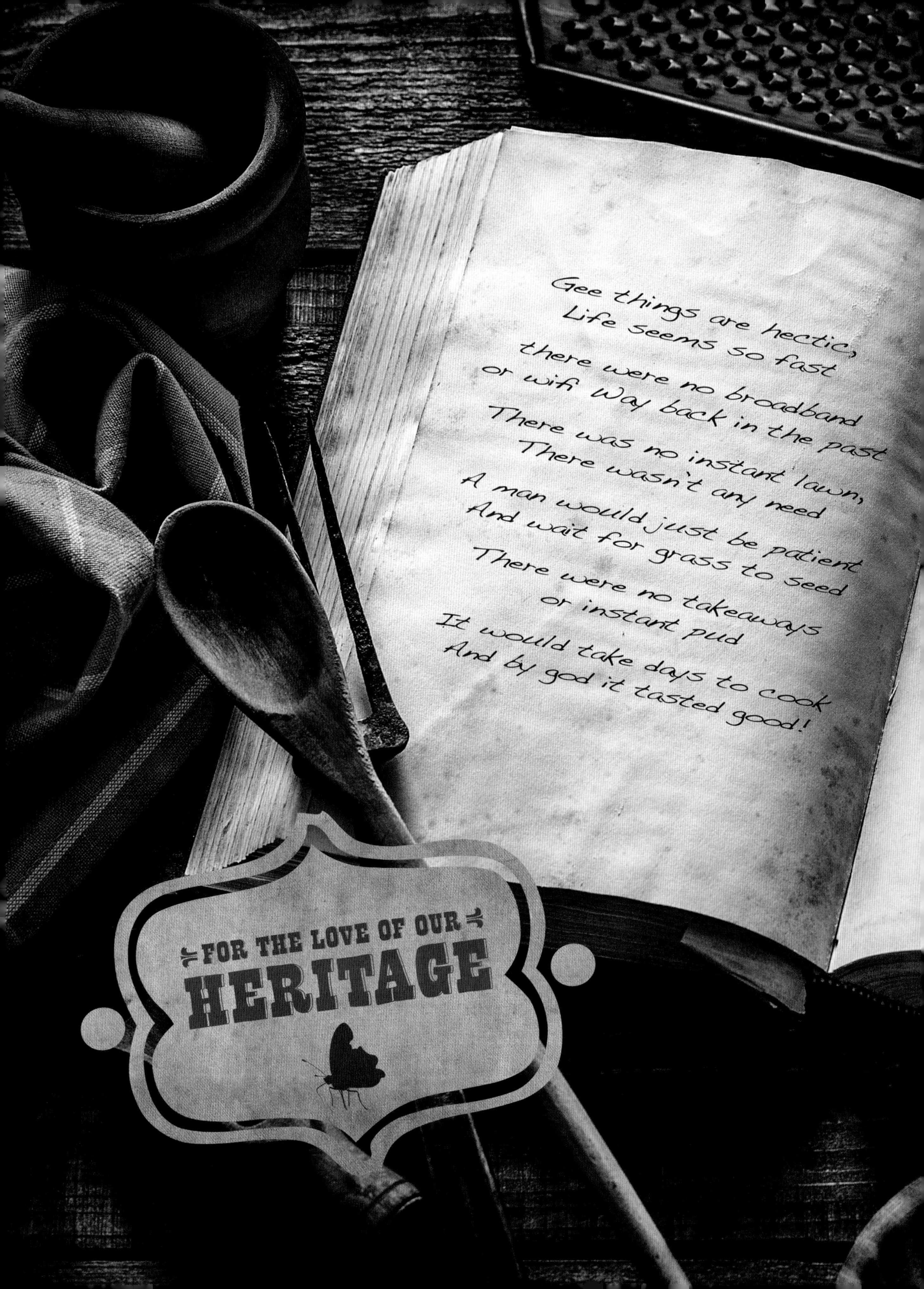
Gee things are hectic,
Life seems so fast
there were no broadband
or wifi Way back in the past
There was no instant lawn,
There wasn't any need
A man would just be patient
And wait for grass to seed
There were no takeaways
or instant pud
It would take days to cook
And by god it tasted good!
FOR THE LOVE OF OUR
HERITAGE

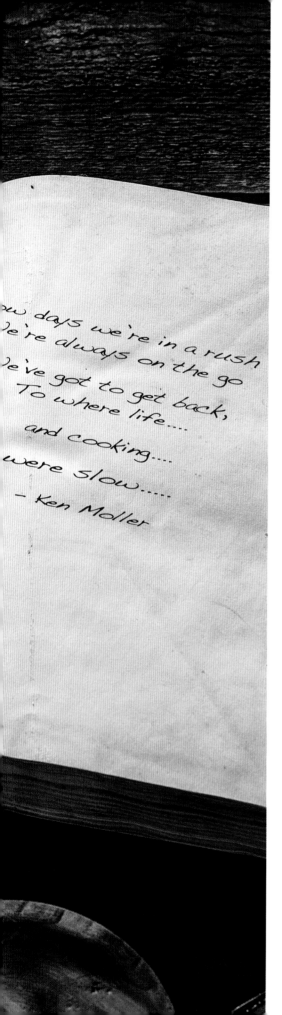

ow days we're in a rush
'e're always on the go
'e've got to get back,
    To where life....
    and cooking....
    were slow.....

    – Ken Moller

OLD
SCHOOL

Jools and I may not be traditionalists, but some
traditions are certainly worth passing on.
As life becomes faster and more stressful, we need
to get back to old-fashioned foods that nourish
and comfort us.
In New Zealand there are so many different food
traditions, we could only choose three.
So given our rural Pakeha background, we visited
three families who epitomise heritage for us:
gathering your own meat, the passing down
of treasured family recipes, and the ancient art
of making honey, one of the original foods humans
have been enjoying for millennia.

JOOLS & BRIDGETTE WERE BIRDS OF A FEATHER WHEN IT CAME TO THEIR SENSE OF HUMOUR

NEW ZEALAND GAME BIRDS

Lynda loves hunting and fishing, providing healthy food for her family, so was thrilled to accept an invitation from Jeff Niblett of NZ Game Birds to join him in the Hawke's Bay for the heritage sport of game-bird shooting. He and his wife Bridgette Karetai have used their combined veterinary skills to raise not only pheasants for organised shoots, but dogs and a gorgeous family too. Bridgette's pheasant pie is destined to be a family heritage recipe, totally delectable.

www.nzgamebirds.co.nz

BRIDGETTE'S
ꞁ PHEASANT PIES ꞁ

MAKES 12 SMALL PIES + PREP TIME 1 HOUR + RESTING + COOK TIME 2 HOURS + COOLING

INGREDIENTS

Pheasant Stock
6 whole pheasants,
    cleaned
4 carrots, roughly chopped
2 onions, halved
4 celery sticks, halved
1 bunch thyme
Small sprig rosemary
Few black peppercorns
2 bay leaves
6 juniper berries, squashed
Pinch of salt

Rough Puff Pastry
225g flour, plus extra for
    rolling
¼ tsp salt
175g butter, not too soft,
    cut in small cubes
150ml ice cold water

Filling
Oil, for cooking
Knob of butter
6 large onions, thinly sliced
4 heaped tbsp wholegrain
    mustard
½ tbsp mustard powder
375ml (half a bottle) white
    wine
Cornflour, for thickening
Lots of picked thyme
    leaves
250g sour cream
Salt and ground black
    pepper, to taste

METHOD

1 To make the Pheasant Stock, place all ingredients in a stockpot,
   top up with water and cook slowly for at least an hour.

2 When meat is tender remove pheasants from pot and strain and
   reserve stock liquid (you will need about 1 litre). Pull the pheasant
   meat from the bones and shred into largish chunks by hand so
   that you can remove any lead shot! Set meat and stock aside.

3 To make the Pie Filling, heat oil and butter in a pot, add onion and
   cook for a few minutes until soft and starting to caramelise. Add
   wholegrain mustard and mustard powder and stir. Increase heat,
   add white wine and about 1 litre of reserved pheasant stock and
   reduce by half. Mix a little cornflour and stock together in a bowl
   and stir through the sauce to thicken it. Add reserved pheasant
   meat, thyme leaves and sour cream, then season to taste with salt
   and pepper. Set aside to cool while you make the pastry.

4 To make the Rough Puff Pastry, place flour and salt in a food
   processor and whizz to combine. Add butter and process until
   the mixture resembles fine breadcrumbs. Add water and pulse
   on high until the dough comes together. Turn out onto a floured
   surface, roll out into a rectangle and fold into 3, turn, roll and fold,
   and repeat 4 times. Wrap in plastic wrap and rest for at least
   15 minutes before use.

5 Preheat oven to 200°C fanbake. Line a 12-hole muffin tin with
   baking paper. Roll out pastry and cut into rounds to line muffin
   tins. Divide filling between the pastry rounds, top each with
   another pastry round and seal the top and bottom pastry edges
   together. Bake for about 20 minutes.

THE BOWMANS

Some families are lucky to have a very special heritage. The Bowmans of Christchurch certainly do. Sarah Bowman's apple shortcake recipe comes from Richard's 'grandma' Hora Doughty, who lived to be 100 and is the great-great-granddaughter of Kamariera Te Hau Takiri Wharepapa, a famous Ngāpuhi chief. Wharepapa, painted by Lindauer in 1895, was one of 14 Māori to travel to England aboard the ship *Ida Zeigler* in 1863. While in England he was presented to Queen Victoria and married a young Englishwoman, Elizabeth Reid. On the journey home the first of their five daughters, Maraea Good Hope Wharepapa, was born. Grandma was named after her grandmother, Wharepapa's daughter Hora Eliza Ann, known as Elizabeth. Wow what a story! And Sarah's apple shortcake had as many delicious layers as her story. And now she has passed it on to her son, William, and given us permission to share it with you.

A STAMP PRINTED BY NEW ZEALAND POST, SHOWS MAORI LEADER TE HAU TAKIRI WHAREPAPA, CIRCA 1980

GRANDMA HORA & HER MOKOPUNA

GRANDMA HORA'S
APPLE SHORTCAKE

SERVES 6 ❖ PREP TIME 20 MINS ❖ COOK TIME 30 MINS

INGREDIENTS

4 large tart apples, peeled, cored and cut into eighths
1 long strip lemon zest
125g butter, softened
½ cup sugar
1 egg
Finely grated zest of 1 lemon
½ cup flour, sifted
1 tsp baking powder, sifted
Icing sugar, to dust

METHOD

1 Preheat oven to 180°C. Set an 11cm x 35cm loose-bottomed tart tin aside.

2 Put apples and lemon zest strip in a pot and half cover with cold water. Cover pot with a lid. Bring to the boil, then reduce heat and simmer for 15 minutes. Drain and set aside.

3 In a large bowl, cream butter and sugar. Add egg and lemon zest and beat until pale and thick. Fold in flour and baking powder.

4 Press half the dough into the base of the tin. Top with apple.

5 Roll remaining dough between two sheets of lightly floured baking paper to form a lid. Cover apple with dough sheet, smoothing any breaks with your fingers.

6 Bake for 25-30 minutes or until golden. Remove from tin and cool on a wire rack. Dust with icing sugar and serve.

GRANDMA HORA'S TIPS

• This is best eaten the day it is made.

• When blackberries are in season, you can use a punnet in place of 2 of the apples, just stew the apples then add fresh or frozen blackberries when assembling.

Reproduced with permission from Cook Simple *by Sarah Bowman. Published by Penguin Group NZ. RRP $45.00.*
Copyright text © Sarah Bowman, 2013.
Copyright photography © Stephen Goodenough, 2013.

DAPHNE'S MUM'S MUM'S
HONEY STEAMED PUDDING

SERVES 8 + PREP TIME 10 MINS + STANDING + COOK TIME 4 HOURS

INGREDIENTS

2 cups flour
½ tsp ground nutmeg
½ tsp mixed spice
½ cup sugar
2 cups sultanas
1 cup dates, halved
½ cup honeydew (or other honey)
1 tsp vanilla essence
1 tbsp butter melted in 1 cup boiling water
2 tsp baking soda stirred into 1 cup cold water
Custard, cream or ice cream, to serve

METHOD

1 Mix flour, spices and sugar together in a steamer bowl. Stir in sultanas and dates.

2 Make a well in the dry ingredients and stir in honey, vanilla essence, then the hot water mixture, then the cold water mixture. Mix well and leave to stand overnight.

3 Next day, wrap up bowl for steaming and steam for 3-4 hours until it smells puddingy. Serve hot with custard, cream or ice cream.

DAPHNE'S MUM'S MUM'S TIPS

- You can steam the pudding immediately rather than leaving it overnight but it's better after overnight standing.

- If making in advance, store in steamer bowl in fridge and reheat by either steaming again for 1 hour or put bowl in slow cooker for 2 -3 hours (the timing isn't critical).

- You could use mixed fruit instead of dates and sultanas.

SYMES HONEY

Staveley in Mid-Canterbury is where Lynda now lives and it just happens to be the honey capital of the South Island. John Symes is a second-generation beekeeper and a legend in the beekeeping world! With the support of his queen bee, Daphne, they've made their life's work the love of bees. And what a small world it is, John tells me that it was our father's brother, Uncle Jim, who gave him NZ's oldest book on beekeeping. He still has it. Daphne shares a precious family heirloom too, her Mum's Mum's steamed pudding made with honeydew. Sticky, runny and yummy.

FOR THE LOVE OF THE
TOPPS

TOPP
⚞ FAMILY ⚟

From the day that we were born, we have been celebrated as twins. Mum didn't know she was having twins so it was a big surprise! We had a charmed childhood, growing up on a Waikato dairy farm in the 1960s. Mum and Dad were always there for us. We had a lot of freedom and learned we could do anything if we put our mind to it.

Dad gave us this beautiful understanding of horses and animals. We had 69 cows and every cow had a name. As we helped him at milking time he'd tell us about the personality of each cow. Those old ways of looking after animals, we learnt from our Dad. He's a really beautiful old farmer. Brother Bruce is generous and funny, the best brother you could ever wish for. He bought us our first guitar. He always wanted to be a floral artist from an early age. He's probably got more artistic genes than both of us put together. No surprise to learn that he's gay as well.

It's true what they say, that home is where the heart is. Mum and Dad sold the farm when they retired and live in Morrinsville now. We wanted to take it over but Dad said 'Go and see the world!'.

We wouldn't change our lives for anything. We've got beautiful parents who are still with us. Our gorgeous brother and his partner Richard. We've always had each other. And now there's also Donna, Lynda's wife, and her two sons, Oliver and Cameron. A loving family is such a blessing. Now that we are so spread out, living all over New Zealand, it is a special time when we get together. And a shared meal with those you love is just magic. It doesn't get any better than that aye?!

NANA'S GINGERNUT BISCUITS

PREP TIME 10 MINS + COOK TIME 20 MINS

INGREDIENTS

125g butter
½ cup golden syrup
½ cup sugar
1½ cups (200g) flour,
   sifted 3 times
1 tsp ground ginger,
   sifted 3 times
½ tsp baking soda,
   sifted 3 times

METHOD

1 Preheat oven to 150°C.

2 Beat butter, golden syrup and sugar together until smooth and creamy. Add dry ingredients and mix well.

3 Take teaspoonfuls of mixture, roll into rounds and space out on a tray. Press flat with a wet finger.

4 Bake for 20 minutes - be careful not to overcook as they burn easily.

OUR MUM, JEAN

Our Mum is just the best baker and home cook in the world and whenever we go home we head straight to the biscuit tin. Mum's gingernuts are legendary and after years of asking, she will finally share her treasured recipe, passed down from our Nana Topp. She still bakes every week, but maybe it's about time we learnt how to make our favourite biscuit ourselves.

JOOLS TOPP

There's something about the smell of a horse – it's like fresh air combined with love and trust. You'd probably be a millionaire if you bottled it and sold it to all those gals out there who miss their equine pals when they're away from home.
I have to blame (or credit) Dad for all my years of horses – he's responsible for getting both Lynda and me hooked as kids – I'm pretty sure it kept us out of trouble as youngsters as well.
He had a cunning plan to keep us occupied with our ponies and it worked, in fact it never went away and today the two of us have nine beautiful horses between us.

I've been lucky enough to study with some great horsemen and horsewomen from the USA who have travelled here to teach – Gwynn Turnbull Weaver, Dr Deb Bennett, Teresa Trull, Buck Brannaman, Martin Black and Dave Weaver. All these great teachers study the old traditions of vaquero horsemanship and classical style.
I've learnt so many great things with all these remarkable people – it's not just a lifestyle, it's is a way of life.
My favourite saying is an old Arabian proverb;

The wind of heaven is that which blows between a horse's ears.

TWO OF MY BEST MATES! INTRIGUE AND WHITE FEATHER MY CAVALIER KING CHARLES SPANIEL

JOOLS'
ONE-EGG
CORN FRITTERS

SERVES 2 + PREP TIME 10 MINS + COOK TIME 10 MINS

INGREDIENTS

400g can creamed
  sweetcorn
1 egg, beaten
1 zucchini, grated
Salt and ground black
  pepper, to taste
3 tbsp flour
½ tbsp baking
  powder
Butter or oil, for
  cooking
Plum or tomato relish,
  to serve

METHOD

1 Place sweetcorn, egg and zucchini in a bowl and mix together.
   Season with salt and pepper.

2 Sift over flour and baking powder and gradually stir in.

3 Heat butter or oil in a frying pan and cook tablespoonfuls of
   mixture until golden on each side. Serve fritters with homemade
   plum or tomato relish.

4   Enjoy, and share with a special friend - aye White Feather?!

LYNDA'S
DUCK BREAST
⊱ PATÉ ⊰

PREP TIME 10 MINS + COOK TIME 20 MINS

INGREDIENTS

Knob of butter
½ onion, finely
 chopped
1 clove garlic, finely
 chopped
1 rasher honey-cured
 bacon, chopped
2 duck breasts
¼ cup red wine, plus
 extra if needed
Blue cheese, to taste
Cracked black pepper,
 to taste

To Serve

Crackers
Cab sav or port

METHOD

1 First go hunting, catch a couple of ducks, clean and chill
 overnight.

2 Melt butter in pan, add onion, garlic and bacon and cook for
 a few minutes, until the onion is soft.

3 Add duck breasts to pan and cook on all sides to seal, then slice,
 add back to pan and cook.

4 Add wine, bubble for about a minute, then remove from heat and
 pour into food processor. Blend until smooth, adding more red
 wine if needed. Crumble in a small amount of blue cheese and
 blend.

5 Place in small containers, crack some black pepper on top and
 chill. Serve with crackers and a cab sav or port.

TOPP LODGE, STAVELEY & MY MATE MOOSE

LYNDA TOPP

Jools and I have the same story because we grew up doing everything together from the time we were conceived. It's quite hard to explain the twin thing. It's a special bond that you have with somebody and it's right there from when you were born. There's always a connection that you know will be there forever. But there is one thing that's a little different; you see Jools missed out on the hunting and fishing gene. I think Dad's got a little gene that he just gave to me.

The first Saturday in May is always a big day on the calendar for me. Nothing can be booked because that is the opening of duck shooting. Opening day is a Kiwi tradition.

A hundred years ago if you wanted a good feed, you'd probably have to go out and hunt it yourself. Going for a hunt to get fresh meat for the table, providing for your family, feels like a real achievement. It makes me feel really proud that I can do this. Also, from a conservation angle, an annual cull of ducks is necessary to maintain a balanced ecosystem, and Fish & Game NZ manage this, making sure not too many ducks are taken in any one place.

I am an advocate for eating what you shoot so all the ducks are retrieved by my trusty old hunting dog Moose. Most of the ducks go into salamis, which are made by our local butcher, but my favourite is the duck breast paté, which I make and share with our neighbours, in front of a roaring fire with a rich red or a tawny port – you can't beat it!

CAMP MOTHER'S
SAUCY TIPS

APPLE SAUCE

Suggestion: Serve with pork chops and deep-fried sage leaves.

INGREDIENTS
4 apples, peeled and
 chopped
2 tbsp lemon juice
1 handful golden raisins
5cm piece ginger, peeled and
 grated
3 tbsp brown sugar
2 cups apple juice
½ tsp ground cinnamon
¼ tsp ground nutmeg

METHOD
1 Combine all ingredients in a pot and cook until a chunky sauce
 forms, about 10-12 minutes.

TZATZIKI

Suggestion: Serve with lamb loin cutlets.

INGREDIENTS
1 medium cucumber
1 clove garlic
1½ tbsp lemon juice
1 tbsp chopped fresh mint
 and dill
1½ cups greek yoghurt
Salt and freshly ground
 pepper, to taste
2 tbsp olive oil

METHOD
1 Peel cucumber, scoop out seeds and grate. Strain cucumber to
 remove all excess liquid. Place drained cucumber in a food
 processor with garlic, lemon juice, dill and mint and process until
 smooth. Stir this mixture into yoghurt and add salt and pepper to
 taste. Whisk in olive oil and season again. Refrigerate for 2 hours
 to allow flavours to combine.

SPICY HOLLANDAISE SAUCE

Suggestion: Serve with grilled salmon.

INGREDIENTS
3 free range egg yolks
A dash of Tabasco sauce
1 tbsp lemon juice
½ tsp lemon zest
Pinch of salt
600g melted butter, hot but
 not boiling
2 tbsp chopped tarragon

METHOD
1 Place egg yolks, Tabasco sauce, lemon juice, lemon zest and salt
 in a food processor and whizz to combine. While the processor is
 running, slowly pour in the butter until it emulsifies and a sauce
 forms. Stir through the tarragon.

CAMP MOTHER'S SAUCY TIPS # 135

PEANUT SAUCE

Suggestion: Serve with venison skewers.

INGREDIENTS
¼ cup creamy peanut butter
1 tsp finely sliced and diced fresh ginger
3 tbsp rice vinegar
3 tsp shaved palm sugar

METHOD
1 Mix all ingredients together in a pot and heat through.

CHEESE FONDUE

Suggestion: Serve with crusty bread and lightly steamed vegetables.

INGREDIENTS
4 cups grated cheese
2 tbsp flour
1 clove garlic, cut in half
1 cup dry white wine
1 tbsp lemon juice
3 tbsp dry sherry or brandy

METHOD
1 Place cheese and flour in a bag and shake until cheese is coated with flour. Rub garlic on bottom and side of fondue pot; discard garlic. Add wine. Heat over simmer setting on fondue pot just until bubbles rise to surface (do not boil). Stir in lemon juice. Gradually add cheese mixture, about ½ cup at a time, stirring constantly with wire whisk over low heat, until melted. Stir in sherry. Keep warm over simmer setting. Fondue must be served over heat to maintain its smooth, creamy texture.

GREEN CHILLI SAUCE

Suggestion: Serve with barbecue prawns.

INGREDIENTS
3 cloves garlic, crushed
3 large green chillies, deseeded and chopped
3 coriander roots, cleaned
3 shallots, finely diced
3 tbsp shaved palm sugar
3 tbsp lime juice
2 tbsp fish sauce

METHOD
1 Place garlic, chillies, coriander roots and shallots in a mortar and pestle and grind together (or whizz together in in a blender). Add palm sugar, lime juice and fish sauce and mix well.

WHIPPED COCONUT CREAM

Suggestion: Serve with saffron meringues.

INGREDIENTS
400ml can coconut cream, chilled in freezer for an hour
1 tsp vanilla essence
1 tbsp liquid honey

METHOD
1 Scoop coconut cream from the can, leaving the watery liquid behind, into a mixing bowl. Whip the coconut cream until thick and peaking. Fold through vanilla and honey.

MUSHROOM & GREEN PEPPERCORN SAUCE

Suggestion: Serve with grilled steak.

INGREDIENTS
2 tbsp olive oil
250g mushrooms, thinly
   sliced
100ml white wine
150ml beef stock
2 tsp green peppercorns in
   brine, drained
1 tsp Dijon mustard
¼ cup cream

METHOD
1 Heat olive oil in a pan. Add mushrooms, cook for a few minutes
   and set aside. Add wine and stock to pan and reduce by half.
   Reduce heat and add peppercorns. Whisk in mustard and cream.
   Return mushrooms to the pan and mix through the sauce to coat.

CREAMY CAPER & GHERKIN SAUCE

Suggestion: Serve with schnitzel and chips.

INGREDIENTS
½ cup sour cream
½ cup mayonnaise
2 hard-boiled free range
   eggs, finely chopped
2-3 gherkins, finely chopped
1 tbsp capers
½ bunch parsley, finely
   chopped
Salt and ground black pepper,
   to taste

METHOD
1 Mix together the sour cream and mayonnaise in a bowl. Fold
   through the eggs, gherkins, capers and parsley. Season with salt
   and pepper to taste.

PEAR & BLACKBERRY SAUCE

Suggestion: Serve with game meats.

INGREDIENTS
1 cup blackberries (frozen is
   fine)
2 pears, cored and thinly
   sliced
4 juniper berries
1 sprig fresh rosemary
2 tbsp red wine vinegar
2 tsp honey

METHOD
1 Place blackberries, pear, juniper berries, rosemary and vinegar in
   a pan and bring to the boil. Turn down and simmer for 20 minutes.
   Remove from heat and add honey.

CAMP MOTHER'S SAUCY TIPS # 139

FOR THE LOVE OF
GOAT

KIDDING AROUND

Most of us Kiwis don't really eat a lot of goat - in fact many of us probably turn our nose up at the thought of it – but all over the world goat is a very popular meat and many countries farm goats in large herds just like we farm sheep in New Zealand. On our journey around NZ we had the chance to sample some amazing recipes cooked up for us by our inspiring *Topp Country* talent and we were pleasantly surprised at how good goat meat tasted.

Not many people know that goats were first introduced to New Zealand around 1773 by James Cook, who liberated English goats into the Marlborough Sounds. Early settlers, explorers and whalers also brought goats with them for food, and used them to barter with Māori. They quickly spread out, forming feral populations that thrived in New Zealand's craggy hills and secluded valleys. Despite an aggressive government culling programme since the 1920s, there is still an abundance of wild goat on our rugged hills and they do a lot of damage.

We now agree wholeheartedly that goat is delicious so it might be time to honour the wily old billy goat and elevate his title to slow-cooked pot roast instead of pest.

WILD GOAT

We've known Pam Hamilton for over 20 years. Every second year in November since 2006, Pam and her team of dedicated locals run the Terrier Race against Time to raise money to support women diagnosed with breast cancer in the Tairawhiti (Gisborne) region. The idea of terrier racing as a fundraiser was started by a group of friends over a bottle of bubbles. Isn't that how all the best ideas start? The committee of six ladies has since raised over $100,000 to date! Incredible! We are only too happy to help and perform at the event when we can.

Feral goats wreak havoc on many New Zealand farms. Pam and her husband, Darcy, often have up to 300 of the little buggers on their farm in Tiniroto near Gisborne at any one time. This is sheep country, but you've got to have the agility of a billy goat to farm it! One goat eats the same amount of grass as one sheep so it's round up time for the wild goats on Kaikino Station. Darcy catches 'em and Pam cooks 'em. Our Dad Peter Topp was born in Gisborne on a small farm in Gray's Bush, and it's always nice to return to his birthplace.

WE ALWAYS FEEL RIGHT AT HOME WITH PAM AND HER FAMILY

PAM'S
⊱ ROAST GOAT ⊰
WITH FIGS & HERBS

SERVES 6 + PREP TIME 10 MINS + COOK TIME 3-4 HOURS

INGREDIENTS

1kg goat leg or shoulder
2 onions, roughly
  chopped
2 oranges, peeled, seeds
  removed and chopped
6-8 fresh figs, halved
2-3 big cloves garlic,
  chopped
1 handful fresh thyme
2 sprigs fresh rosemary
330ml can beer
Salt and ground black
  pepper, to taste

METHOD

1 Preheat oven to 150°C or set slow-cooker to high. Place all
   ingredients in lidded roasting dish or large camp oven or
   slow-cooker dish.

2 Cook, covered, in the oven or slow-cooker for 3-4 hours or
   until the meat is fork tender. If you're cooking in the oven you'll
   need to check a few times to stir and make sure there's
   enough liquid. Don't lift the lid off your slow-cooker –
   1 can of beer will provide plenty of liquid.

PAMS TIPS

• It's important that you don't treat goat meat as you would
  lamb. Goat meat is lean with little fat, so it will toughen up if
  cooked at high temperatures without moisture.

• Don't serve it rare. It should be cooked thoroughly otherwise
  it will be tough.

• Younger goat is much tastier – don't cook an old billy.

WILD GOATS, TINIROTO.

KEN'S
⇒ POEM ⇒

WHEN FOLKS WILL TELL YOU
YOU'RE ACTING LIKE A GOAT,

DOES THIS MEAN YOU'RE
BUTTING THINGS?
AND EATING GRANDMA'S COAT?

THE BILLY GOAT IS RUGGED
AND A LITTLE ON THE SMELLY SIDE

BUT HE MAKES A DAMN GOOD CURRY
AND YOU CAN ALSO TAN HIS HIDE

THE NANNY GOAT IS SWEET
HER MILK AND CHEESE DIVINE

BUT IF YOU TURN YOUR BACK
SHE'LL EAT YOUR UNDIES OFF
THE LINE!

(AND THE ONES YOU'RE
WEARING TOO)

THREE LITTLE BIRDS' CURRY GOAT

SERVES 6 + PREP TIME 30 MINS + COOK TIME 1½ HOURS

INGREDIENTS

1.5kg goat meat
2 tbsp water
2 tbsp white vinegar
1 onion, chopped
2 spring onions, chopped
4 cloves garlic, chopped
1 tsp chopped fresh
    ginger
2 tsp chopped thyme
2 tbsp ground turmeric
½ scotch bonnet or
    habanero chilli pepper,
    chopped
1 tsp salt
2 tbsp curry powder
¼ cup vegetable oil
4 cups boiling water
1 large white potato,
    peeled and diced
1 carrot, peeled and sliced
4 whole pimento berries
    (allspice), crushed

METHOD

1 Trim excess fat from meat, cut it into bite-sized pieces and
   wash in a mixture of water and vinegar. Place in a bowl.

2 Add onion, spring onion, garlic, ginger, thyme, turmeric,
   scotch bonnet or habanero, salt and half of the curry powder
   to the bowl. Rub the seasonings into the meat, cover the bowl
   and set aside to marinate for 2 hours.

3 Heat vegetable oil in a heavy-bottomed pan over a medium
   heat and add the remaining curry powder. Add the marinated
   meat and sear on all sides. Add boiling water. Cover and
   allow to simmer for about 1 hour 20 minutes, or until the meat
   is tender.

4 Add the potato and cook for 5 minutes. Fold in the carrot and
   pimento berries and cook for 5 minutes.

5 Serve with desired accompaniments such as cooked white
   jasmine rice, boiled green bananas, vegetable salad and
   mango chutney.

TOPP TIP

• To sear is to brown meat quickly by subjecting it to very high
  heat either in a skillet, under a grill or in a very hot oven. The
  object of searing is to seal in the meat's juices.

THREE LITTLE BIRDS

From Kingston, Jamaica to Petone, Wellington, Simon and Alecia Cole-Bowen are a long way from their friends and family. They met at a bus stop in Spanish Town, St Catherine and quickly fell in love and got married. After studying and working in the United States for some time they decided they needed a better way of life for their kids.

One Sunday afternoon after dinner Alecia went on her laptop and googled "where's the best place to live in the world and raise a family?" New Zealand came up and she was blown away by the beauty. They love living here and keep the taste of home close with their famous curry goat.

Goat is the king of meat in Jamaica and these two are so passionate about sharing this delicacy they can be found every Friday at the Cuba Street night markets as Three Little Birds Catering. Their jerk chicken and pork might be popular but it's their curry goat that's the star of the show!

www.facebook.com/tlbcatering

SARAH'S
GOATS' CHEESE
WITH COINTREAU DRIZZLE

INGREDIENTS

150g butter
Cointreau, to taste
1 whole Tenara Goats'
    Cheese (ash-coated
    goats' cheese)

To Serve
Fresh seasonal local fruit
Nuts
Lavosh crackers

METHOD

1 Heat a pot over a medium heat. Add butter, allow to melt and and add Cointreau to taste.

2 Place Tenara Goats' Cheese on a serving platter and pile fresh fruit, nuts and crackers around it. Drizzle over the Cointreau sauce just before serving.

SARAH'S TIP

• If you don't have any Cointreau you could reduce orange juice by half and add honey to desired sweetness.

KAIKOURA CHEESE

Daniel and Sarah Jenkins and their daughters Pipi and Coya are just mad about goats and after only a few years making their Kaikoura Cheese, the company is making a BIG name for itself. This lovely family is raising a beautiful herd of goats in the hills of Kaikoura. It's been a rollercaster ride for the young family - the family was living in Christchurch until the earthquake in 2011. The quake was the catalyst to Daniel and Sarah making their dream of Kaikoura Cheese a reality.

The subsequent earthquake that hit Kaikoura in 2016 has left them "shaken, but not stirred". It will clearly be a while before things are back to normal, but while the earthquake has undoubtedly presented a huge challenge, it is one that they have accepted with a determination to not only survive, but to come back better and stronger!

www.kaikouracheese.co.nz

FOR THE LOVE OF
FRUIT

A LITTLE
⊰ FRUITY ⊱

The tree I most remember growing up was a beautiful old Black Doris plum tree right smack bang in the middle of the horse paddock. It was so precious that Dad had built a big fence around it so the polo ponies wouldn't rub up against it, or eat the fruit.

When the plums were ready, Mum would cut them up into slices, dust lightly with icing sugar and put them in the fridge to chill.

We would have them for dessert with freshly whipped cream from the cowshed. This was a heavenly taste for such a simple treat that required no cooking at all.

Mum did cook one fruit that grew in the orchard and that became a staple in our school lunch boxes – stewed tamarillos, known as tree tomatoes when we were growing up.

Once stewed with a little sugar and water and then chilled, she put them in a small Agee jar with two crushed Weet-Bix and pouring cream over the top, screwed the lid on and sent us off to school.

Most days we ate it on the bus in the morning. Other kids tried to swap their lunch with us so they could try it, it rarely ever made it to lunchtime.

Lynda and I also spent a good long time just sitting in that tree eating as many tamarillos as we could. To this day they are our favourite fruit.

COUNTRY TRADING COMPANY

Heather and Andrew Cole met 25 years ago through a pair of socks: while on a tramping trip together in Kaikoura he lent her a dry pair, which he kept coming back to pick up but forgetting! A love affair began and continues to flourish today. They've weathered her terrible 1980s perm, being separated for four years while she studied in Otago (they wrote every week), and they spent five years in London working in the high tech and corporate sectors, which saw them flying all over the world – Russia, Riyadh, Istanbul, Silicon Valley... In 2004, vowing to leave the corporate world behind, they returned to New Zealand in search of their dream to live a simple and self-reliant life. They found a beautiful lifestyle block outside Nelson, planted 140 fruit trees and, discovering how hard it was to source quality, practical supplies for their kitchen and garden, started the Country Trading Company. Since then they have developed a range of products to help other growers and makers in their down-to-earth endeavours. They live by the maxim "have less, enjoy more". The day we visited Heather she had made everything on the generous platter of fruits, cheese, breads and paste. Andrew is also a craft beer maker and together with David Watson owns and runs NZ's oldest pub, The Moutere Inn. Talk about a genius move home!

www.countrytrading.co

HEATHER'S
❧ DAMSON PASTE ☙

PREP TIME 20 MINS + COOK TIME ABOUT 35 MINS

INGREDIENTS

500g damsons
1 cup cider
5 cloves
About 250g sugar

METHOD

1 Lightly grease moulds with a mild-flavoured cooking oil such as rice bran or grapeseed oil and set aside.

2 Place damsons in a stainless steel pot, add cider and cloves and cook until very soft and a little reduced (about 5 minutes).

3 Push the damson pulp through a sieve or mouli to remove the stones. Weigh the pulp and put it in a heavy-bottomed high-sided frying pan with half the weight of the pulp in sugar. Boil, stirring frequently. It will be ready when you can draw a wooden spoon across the pan and the line won't join up. This can take up to 30 minutes.

4 Pour it into the prepared moulds, smooth the surface and set it aside to set. When set and cold, turn out the moulds and wrap in greaseproof paper. Store in an airtight container on a cool shelf.

CAROLANN'S
⚜ BLUEBERRY ⚜
BUTTERMILK PANCAKES

SERVES 4 + PREP TIME 20 MINS + COOK TIME 15 MINS

INGREDIENTS

2 cups flour
¼ cup sugar
2¼ tsp baking powder
½ tsp baking soda
½ tsp salt
2 eggs
2 cups buttermilk or milk
¼ cup melted unsalted butter, plus extra for frying
1 cup blueberries

To Serve
Whipped cream
Maple syrup

METHOD

1   In a large bowl sift together the flour, sugar, baking powder, baking soda and salt.

2   Beat the eggs with the buttermilk and melted butter. Combine the dry and the wet ingredients into a lumpy batter, being careful not to over-mix (see Tip).

3   Heat some butter in a skillet over a medium heat. Spoon ⅓ cup of batter into the skillet and sprinkle the top with some of the blueberries. Cook for 2-3 minutes on each side.

4   Serve with a dollop of whipped cream and maple syrup.

CAROLANN'S TIP

●   Don't over-mix the batter – if you do you'll get flat, heavy pancakes.

SUSTAINABLE LIVING & BLUEBERRIES

Carolann Murray was once a night-clubbing city slicker who traded in her high heels for gumboots. She headed for the hills just outside of Wellington and now she's putting the self back into self-sufficiency. From honey collecting to alternative energy, Carolann's life is jam-packed – just like her pantry! We gorged ourselves silly on her incredible giant blueberries and learnt how to turn cream into fuel to run the cutest little tractor we've ever had the pleasure to drive. This woman is a superwoman!

GIANT BLUEBERRIES AND A TRACTOR THAT RUNS ON GHEE – WHAT MORE COULD A GIRL WANT!?

LOTHLORIEN FEIJOAS

Lothlorien is a magical land filled with elves and hobbits and bearded men. But this is no fairytale. With eight children and 16 grandchildren between them, Dale DeMeulemeester and Jo Bradshaw have created their very own paradise at their Lothlorien Feijoa Winery near Warkworth, 100 acres of magic where children and adults run free and the organic feijoa wine runs even freer. Dale is originally from Detroit and as he puts it, "If you've ever been to Detroit then you'll know it's a good place to leave".

40 years ago he fell in love with a trifecta that would change his life: New Zealand, his Australian partner (Jo), and feijoas, and together he and Jo created the farm, and a family, that is still at the centre of their lives. All of their children were born there, and even though they've all gone away every one has come back and they are all involved in the feijoa wine-making process.

www.lothlorienwinery.co.nz

JO'S
⊰ FEIJOA SELF SAUCING PUDDING ⊱

SERVES 6 ✦ PREP TIME 20MINS ✦ COOK TIME 30 MINS

INGREDIENTS

125g butter
¾ cup brown sugar
2 eggs
½ cup white flour
½ cup wholemeal
   flour
2 tsp baking powder
1 tsp vanilla
2 cups feijoa pulp
   mixed with 2 tbsp
   brown sugar

METHOD

1 Preheat oven to 180°C and lightly grease a 20cm cake tin.

2 Cream the butter and sugar together in a bowl. Mix in the eggs, one at a time, beating in about 1 tsp of the flour after each egg to prevent the mixture from curdling. Fold through remaining flour and baking powder. Mix in vanilla.

3 Pour batter into the prepared cake tin. Pour over feijoa pulp and sugar mixture. Bake for 30 minutes.

JO'S TIP

• You can add a little milk or cream when you're adding the vanilla if you have some to hand.

KEN'S POEM

THE GRANNY SMITH AT ITS BEST
IS CRISP
IT MAKES A SCRUMPTIOUS PIE

AND IF YOU LOVE SOMEONE DEARLY
THEY'RE THE APPLE OF YOUR EYE

BANANA, PEACH AND MELONS
A LUSCIOUS FRUIT AFFAIR

BUT MY FAVOURITE, KEN
IS A LOVELY JUICY PEAR

THERE ARE MANY DIFFERENT
KINDS OF FRUITS

SOME GROW ON TREES
AND SOME WEAR SUITS...

FOR THE LOVE OF THE
EXOTIC

TASTE BUD TOURISM

The definition of exotic is "originating in or characteristic of a distant foreign country" and also "attractive or striking because colourful or out of the ordinary". Food can also have these attributes and the more exotic we throw at our taste buds, the more we open up a world of sensational, extravagant, bizarre, fantastic, curious, different and unfamiliar culinary delights.

Growing up in rural New Zealand in the 60s and 70s didn't exactly set our taste buds alight. Avocados were not widely available until the 80s and were considered "exotic". How far we have come in a few decades! We encourage you to be adventurous and experience foods and taste sensations you have yet to try. So go on don't be afraid, put aside your meat-and-three- veg dinner or your scones and jam and try something exotic – it may help us to understand different cultures a little better and make us more courageous.

KOWHAI GROVE OSTRICH FARM

Ian and Rosemary Blunden are leading New Zealand's ostrich farming charge on their Kowhai Grove Farm in the Manawatu with about 300 ostriches, bred for their meat and leather. These elegant birds lay the largest eggs in the world and make a damn delicious burger.

Who knew that one ostrich egg has as much egg in it as 24 hen's eggs? Ostrich meat is very red, low in cholesterol and fat, and very high in iron - it mostly comes from the legs and behind, and is great on the barbecue. Ostriches are the largest and fastest birds on earth. Their powerful, long legs can also be formidable weapons, capable of killing a human or a potential predator such as a lion with a forward kick, so we made sure to give these birds a wide berth, apart from the chicks, which we wanted to take home! Contrary to popular belief, ostriches do not bury their heads in the sand: the myth probably originates from the bird's defensive behaviour of lying low at the approach of trouble and pressing their long necks to the ground in an attempt to become less visible.

www.kowhaigroveostrich.co.nz

ROSEMARY'S OSTRICH STEAK & EGG BURGERS

SERVES 6 + PREP TIME 10 MINS + REST TIME + COOK TIME 10 MINS

INGREDIENTS

465g ostrich eye fillet
Olive oil
1 ostrich egg (or 18
  hen's eggs)
Salt and ground black
  pepper, to taste

To Serve
Burger buns
Beetroot relish
Lettuce

METHOD

1   Slice ostrich eye fillet into six 1-1.5cm thick medallions. Rub a little olive oil into both sides and leave to rest for 30-60 minutes at room temperature.

2   Heat a pan over a high heat and sear ostrich medallions quickly on both sides, remove from pan, cover and rest for 5 minutes. Ostrich meat is at its best cooked medium rare.

3   Whisk egg with salt and pepper, add to pan and scramble gently.

4   Assemble burgers with buns, ostrich medallions, egg, beetroot relish and lettuce.

WHANGARIPO BUFFALO

These beautiful beasts usually roam the swamps of exotic lands far away. But thanks to Annie Wills and Phil Armstrong you can now find them roaming on farmlands in the Whangaripo Valley near Matakana, where they produce buffalo cheese. Buffalo milk is commonly drunk all over the world, especially in Iran and India. Buffalo milk has two-and-a-half times the milk solids of cow's milk, with 4.5 per cent protein, 8 per cent fat, higher calcium, the same lactose (sugar) but only half the cholesterol. It is also all A2 protein, not A1 (like most cow's milk) and people with lower levels of dairy intolerance are often able to consume buffalo milk products quite happily. Buffalo ooze with personality and so do this fabulous family. They're the perfect farming match!

BUFFALO MOZZARELLA GRATIN

SERVES 2 AS AN ENTRÉE + PREP TIME 5 MINS + COOK TIME 8 MINS.

INGREDIENTS

½ cup dry breadcrumbs

2 sprigs fresh thyme, chopped

Zest of 1 lemon

1 tsp ground black pepper

2 balls fresh buffalo mozzarella, torn into pieces

2 tbsp olives, sliced

Salt and ground black pepper, to taste

2 tbsp olive oil

Bread, to serve

METHOD

1 Preheat the oven grill.

2 In a small bowl, mix the breadcrumbs, thyme, lemon zest and black pepper. Set aside.

3 Divide the buffalo mozzarella pieces between 2 small ovenproof serving dishes or place in 1 large dish. Sprinkle over olives and season. Top with the seasoned breadcrumb mixture.

4 Drizzle the olive oil over the top and place under the grill until bubbling and the breadcrumb mixture is golden brown, about 5-8 minutes. Serve immediately with bread.

GRASSHOPPERS

Edible insects are the future of food according to the United Nations. Meet the wild and whacky family leading the gastronomic bug movement in New Zealand.

Back in the days of old, Hokitika was the gold rush capital of New Zealand. These days people are more likely to be seen rushing to the annual Wildfoods Festival. And the star attraction? The Crouching Grasshopper stall! Fiona Anderson is passionate about feeding people exotic bugs and serves around a 1000 of the critters each year! Her interest in eating bugs began when a friend from Cambodia gave her a recipe. In a lot of Asian countries eating insects is totally normal and they are very high in nutrients. Fiona's husband Liam hates bugs. His Hungarian langos foodtruck serves up an exotic treat of the ACTUALLY delicious kind.

FIONA'S
⅊ FRIED GRASSHOPPERS ⅃
WITH SATAY SAUCE

SERVES 6 AS AN ENTREE ⁜ PREP TIME 30 MINS ⁜ COOK TIME 10 MINS

INGREDIENTS

Oil, for deep-frying
6 frozen grasshoppers

Satay Sauce *(makes 1 cup)*
Oil, for cooking
2 tbsp finely chopped
  onion
1 small clove garlic, finely
  chopped
½ cup crunchy peanut
  butter
½ cup water
2 tbsp sweet chilli sauce
1 tbsp soy sauce
Squeeze of lemon or lime
  juice, to taste

To Serve
½ cup steamed rice
6 red cabbage leaves
  (large enough to roll
  around a spoonful of
  rice)

METHOD

1 To make the Satay Sauce, heat a dash of oil in a small pot. Cook
   onion and garlic over a low heat until soft. Add peanut butter and
   water. Mix until combined and smooth. Remove from heat and stir
   in sweet chilli sauce, soy sauce and lemon or lime juice. Set aside.

2 Heat oil for deep-frying in a frypan or wok to a high temperature.
   Drop frozen grasshoppers in hot oil and cook until golden brown
   in colour – they will cook and change colour quickly so don't turn
   away! Set aside to drain excess oil while cooking the rest.

3 To serve put a spoonful of steamed rice on each red cabbage leaf.
   Drizzle over a spoonful of satay sauce. Place a fried grasshopper
   on top, roll up the cabbage leaf and eat (go on, dare ya!).

HOKITIKA SUNSET

FOR THE LOVE OF
SPICE

SPICE OF
≈ LIFE ≈

When we were growing up on the farm I can only remember three spicy dishes. One of them was curried mince with sultanas – yuck (ha,ha sorry Mum, that wasn't one of your finest). The other two were curried eggs, which had the same curry mixture in as the mince and were always popular.

The last one was Lynda's and my favourite pudding. Nana Topp's apple pie - it had about six layers of sliced apple, sugar, sultanas and cinnamon, and was served hot with fresh poured cream from the cows.

There was no sign of garlic, fennel, turmeric, star anise or (heaven forbid) chilli, in the family kitchen.

But times have changed and most of these amazing spices are now staple supplies in many New Zealand kitchen cupboards.

We first got our taste for hot and spicy food while performing in Melbourne in the '80s – we got to try a Malaysian laksa, which is a spicy coconut soup with either veggies, chicken or fish. It's now an absolute favourite and wherever we go we always try to seek out a good laksa.

Our advice to 'spice virgins' is to start mild and work your way up to hot, believe me the taste sensation will grow on you if you take the plunge.

Hey - I forgot one more spice that Mum always used... there was always a little packet of Gregg's Ground Ginger for her best treat - and featured in this book - Nana Topp's Gingernuts (see page 126).

JOOLS & HOPE MEYER SHARE A SPECIAL CONNECTION. LYNDA'S CHILLI CONNECTION BROUGHT HER TO TEARS!

FIRE DRAGON CHILLIES

Clint and Libby Meyer reckon the key to a spicy life is keeping it simple. After many years travelling around the world, with Clint on a personal mission to eat the hottest chillies he could find, they came home and settled on a beautiful piece of land near the Hokianga Harbour. In the Northland sub-tropical climate, they grow a range of chillies from imported and cross-bred seed organically and with no sprays or additives. Their award-winning range of Fire Dragon Chilli sauces now has an international cult following. And it's not just chillies they breed: they also have three awesome kids. Clint is crazy about chillies. He eats them at least three times a day. His promise of an endorphin rush got Lynda excited, so she had a crack at eating a Carolina Reaper - the world's hottest chilli (and cried) while Jools got to hang out with the world's cutest kid.

www.firedragonchillies.co.nz

LIBBY'S
⊱ DELHI DAHL ⊰

SERVES 4-5 ✦ PREP TIME 10 MINS ✦ COOK TIME 50 MINS

INGREDIENTS

¼ cup oil/ghee/butter
4 cloves garlic
2 large onions
3 fresh chillies
   (optional, see Tip)
2 tsp ground turmeric
2 tbsp ground
   coriander
1 tbsp ground cumin
300g red lentils
2 tbsp tomato paste
¼ cup tomato sauce
1.5 litres vegetable or
   chicken stock
Salt and ground black
   pepper, to taste
5 boiled eggs

METHOD

1 Heat the oil, ghee or butter in a pot and cook the garlic, onion, chillies, if using, and spices until lightly browned, about 5 minutes. Add the lentils, tomato paste and tomato sauce and stir through until well combined. Add stock and bring to the boil. Season to taste.

2 Turn down the heat and simmer, stirring occasionally, for 35-45 minutes until the lentils start to fall apart. Add the boiled eggs to the pot 10 minutes before the end of cooking time.

3 Serve with desired accompaniments: we like Fire Dragon Chilli sauce, yoghurt, fresh herbs and flaked almonds.

LIBBY'S CHILLI TIP

● We often omit the chillies because of the kids, then just add our own hot sauces to our own dishes.

TANAH'S
LA YOU CHILLI OIL

MAKES ABOUT 2 CUPS + PREP 5 MINS + COOK TIME 5 MINS

INGREDIENTS

2 tbsp red chilli
  powder
2 tbsp dried red chilli
  flakes
2 dried red chilli
1 tbsp light soy sauce
1 tbsp Shaoxing wine
  or dry sherry or
  whiskey
1 cinnamon quill
2 whole star anise
2 cups peanut oil
  (canola or
  sunflower oil can
  be used)
1 tablespoon dried
  shrimp (optional)

METHOD

1 In a large heatproof dish, add all the dry ingredients together. Mix in soy sauce and Shaoxing wine and set aside.

2 In a small pot, heat oil till it's very hot, then carefully pour the hot oil in the heatproof dish together with the other ingredients. Mix while the oil is sizzling and bubbling. Let it sit overnight to allow the flavours to infuse together. Use liberally for a spice kick!

Every street food vendor, canteen and restaurant has their own secret recipe La You chilli oil offered alongside the staple seasonings of soy sauce and black rice vinegar. They are the salt and pepper equivalents in many Chinese establishments. It's easy to prepare – keep in a sealed glass jar up to 3 months in a dark cupboard.

ORIENTAL SPICE

Kiwis love Asian food. From Chinese to Thai, it's NZ's biggest dining-out experience but, sadly and unnecessarily, most of us are a bit shy about shopping at the Asian supermarkets, such as Tai Ping Market in Dominion Road, Auckland, where you can find just about everything from fresh home-made dumplings to roasted duck and all the ingredients for the two delicious dishes that Tanah Dowdle and Freddy Sy taught us to cook. The Asian markets are both fascinating and exciting, so go on, give them a go! Tanah and Freddy run Asian-inspired food tours and cooking classes in Auckland. You can find them on www.facebook.com/gourmetjoy

JOOLS DISCOVERS HER INNER CHICKEN & WE LEARN THE SECRETS OF SZECHUAN COOKING

FREDDY'S
⇥ DAN DAN NOODLES ⇤

SERVES 2-3 + PREP TIME 10 MINS + COOK TIME 15 MINS

Dan Dan Noodles are a super popular street food in China. The cook balances baskets and stove over their shoulder on a bamboo pole. Call out your order and they squat down and create Dan Dan Noodles right in front of you. We have added a delicious vegetarian option as well.

INGREDIENTS

Noodles
500g fresh la mein noodles wheat noodles or fresh spaghetti noodles or dry egg noodles

Dan Dan Sauce
500g ground pork or beef or substitute with chopped brown or field mushrooms
1 tbsp peanut oil
1 tbsp garlic (about 3 cloves), minced
1 tbsp fresh ginger, minced
2 spring onions thinly sliced - white part only, green part as a topping
2 tbsp Shaoxing rice wine or substitute with dry sherry or whiskey
1 tbsp light soy sauce
2 tbsp Chinese sweet bean paste or substitute with hoisin sauce
2 tbsp oyster sauce

Dressing
½ cup chicken stock or water
¼ cup light soy sauce
3 tbsp Chinese sesame paste or tahini or peanut butter
2 tbsp Chinese black rice vinegar or balsamic vinegar
1 tbsp sesame oil
1 tbsp sugar or honey
½ tsp toasted, ground Szechuan pepper

Toppings
1 cup dry-roasted peanuts, finely chopped
2 tbsp Chinese preserved mustard greens/ vegetables, chopped (optional)
2 spring onions - green part - thinly sliced

Toppings cont...
A pinch per bowl of Szechuan peppercorn (gently toasted until fragrant in dry pan and finely pounded)
La You Chilli Oil drizzle to taste (see page 174)

METHOD

1 To prepare the dressing, put the sesame paste in a bowl, slowly whisk in the wet ingredients a little at a time to get a smooth even consistency. Set aside.

2 Transfer each topping to their own individual bowls. Set aside.

3 Heat a large wok or skillet over medium-high heat. Add the oil, garlic, ginger, white parts of the spring onions, fry for 30 seconds. Add the meat or mushrooms and fry until brown. Add Shaoxing wine to deglaze the pan. Next add sweet bean paste, oyster sauce and soy sauce and cook for a further minute. Keep warm.

4 Take your largest pot, fill with lots of salted water, bring to rolling boil. Cook the noodles (note: do not overcook). Immediately strain and serve noodles into individual bowls.

5 Arrange Dan Dan sauce, dressing and toppings on the table. Assemble your bowl of noodles to suit your taste and mix well. For that authentic kick, be bold with a swirl of La You Chilli Oil and a pinch of Szechuan pepper. Mix well and enjoy with a cold glass of beer!

TURMERIC

Nestled in the Northland bush of Matapouri, landscape designer Russell Fransham and his partner McGregor Smith created a magical wonderland at their Subtropicals nursery, which also grows a range of exotic plants for use in creating spicy culinary masterpieces including galangal, ginger, garlic, lemongrass and turmeric.

Sadly, Russell passed away suddenly in December 2017. One of the most respected figures in New Zealand horticulture, and an authority on adapting unusual and subtropical plants to New Zealand conditions, Russell has left an amazing legacy behind. He is very much missed not only by Mac and his family, but also the Matapouri community and New Zealand's horticultural world. We feel very lucky to have met him.

"I knew Russell as a kind, intelligent human being with a great love for the natural world. In our frequent travels, he showed himself to be open to difference, was inspired by the environment, and in turn was inspirational to others when creating their gardens. One of Russell's catchphrases was 'Dare to be different'. And he lived by this. He pushed the boundaries with his landscaping, tested the margins and, due to his eye for detail and artistry, always produced work with a uniqueness. Through endless investigations and a lifetime of experience, Russell developed incredible knowledge and was generous in sharing it to benefit others. He had a passion for growing food and encouraged anyone who had at least a bucket of dirt to jump on this bandwagon and grow, grow, grow. Not only will you enjoy the fruits of your labour, but the process keeps you connected to the earth. One of the things that Russell would like to be remembered for is creating beautiful spaces that live on for generations to enjoy. Thanks for our wonderful life together." Mac

DID YOU KNOW?

GALANGAL: Galangal is part of the ginger family and it is native to Thailand, China and Indonesia. It has been cultivated in China from before 1000 AD. It is believed to aid digestion, reduce inflammation, support brain health and improve sperm count. No wonder German philosopher Hildegard of Bingen called galangal "the spice of life" in the late 11th century!

GINGER: Ginger is a rhizome, not a root, and you can grow them from the rhizomes found at grocery stores, so long as you live somewhere warm enough. Ginger is actually classified as a herb and is grown in tropical areas around the world. In Greece, folk would eat ginger wrapped in bread to treat digestive problems. Eventually ginger was added to the bread dough and, you guessed it, that worldwide favourite, gingerbread, was born! Ginger is an excellent natural remedy for nausea, motion sickness, morning sickness and general tummy upsets.

GARLIC: Garlic is packed with vitamins and minerals including potassium, iron, calcium, magnesium, manganese, zinc, selenium, beta-carotene and vitamin C. The use of garlic in cooking and for good health dates all the way back to the ancient Egyptian pharaohs, Greeks, Chinese and Babylonians. Garlic is used to combat everything from the common cold to high blood pressure and some claim it can help reduce the risk of common brain diseases such as Alzheimer's and dementia. Makes that delicious buttery garlic bread look even better aye?

MAC'S
TURMERIC TARAKIHI

SERVES 4 + PREP TIME 10 MINS + MARINATING + COOK TIME 10 MINS

INGREDIENTS

4 fish fillets
Oil, for cooking
6 thin slices galangal
1 onion, thinly sliced
1 handful fresh dill
2-3 spring onions tops, chopped

Marinade

3-4 tbsp Vietnamese fish sauce
1 dsp ground turmeric
1-2 tbsp crushed garlic
½ tbsp crushed ginger
2 shallots, finely diced
½ tsp ground black pepper
2 tbsp finely chopped dill

To Serve

Cooked vermicelli noodles
Finely chopped chilli
Chopped spring onion greens
1 handful cashews
Dipping sauce (optional)

METHOD

1 Place all the Marinade ingredients in a bowl and mix to combine. Add the fish fillets and rub the marinade into the fish fillets thoroughly. Set aside to marinate for 2 hours, turning fillets from time to time to make sure all the surfaces are covered.

2 Heat a little oil in a pan. Add galangal and cook in the oil. When the galangal is cooked remove from oil with a slotted spoon and discard, leaving the flavoured oil in the pan.

3 Add onion to oil and fry lightly. Add dill and spring onion and sauté. Remove from pan and keep warm.

4 Using the same flavoured oil, quickly pan-fry the fillets of fish, carefully turning only once.

5 To serve, divide vermicelli noodles between plates, top with the onion and dill mixture and then the fish fillets. Sprinkle over chilli, spring onion greens and cashews and serve with a dipping sauce, if desired.

GOLDEN TURMERIC LATTE
⇒ FOR TWO ⇒

SERVES 2 ✦ PREP TIME 5 MINS ✦ COOK TIME 5 MINS

INGREDIENTS

2-3 cups almond milk (or any milk of your choice)

1-2 tsp grated fresh turmeric or ½ tsp ground turmeric

1 tsp grated fresh ginger or ½ tsp ground ginger

½ tsp ground cinnamon, plus extra to serve

½ tsp vanilla extract

1 tsp maple syrup

ground black pepper, to taste

METHOD

1 Place all ingredients in a pot and whisk constantly over a gentle heat. Once hot, pour into mugs and sprinkle with a little more cinnamon to serve.

BENEFITS OF TURMERIC

Turmeric takes centre stage as one of the most beneficial spices in the world and is thought of as holy in India. It has been positively linked to helping combat cancer, kidney and cardiovascular diseases, arthritis, and irritable bowel disease, Alzheimer's disease and diabetes. We should all be eating turmeric every day!

KEN'S POEM

OLD SPICE DEODORANT
NOW THAT'S WHAT I CALL HOT

ALWAYS HAD MEAT AND VEG
IN MY COOKING POT

SPICES, CHILLI, GARLIC
THERE'S SO MUCH MORE TO CHOOSE

THEY'VE EVEN GOT THE ZEST
OF ORANGE IN MY LOCAL BOOZE.

DON'T GET ME WRONG I'LL HAVE A
CRACK AT ANYTHING YOU MAKE

ONCE AT A FANCY RESTAURANT
I HAD A PEPPERED STEAK.

YOU'VE GOT TO BRANCH OUT BOY
GET YOUR TASTE BUDS UP TO DATE

HAVE A SPICY LAKSA OR A VINDALOO
THAT'LL GET YOUR JUICES
RUNNING MATE,

BOTH ENDS.

FOR THE LOVE OF
FLOWERS

FLOWER POWER

Our brother Bruce is a fully trained and talented florist – he was even the president of Interflora for several years. He has created some of the most beautiful wedding flowers, bouquets and arrangements known to man - or woman. Mum and Bruce worked together at their Huntly florist shop for many years and they sent flowers all over the world.

All sorts of emotions can be observed when people receive these floral gifts but not many people associate flowers as being something to appease our hunger pains. Who knew many flowers are in fact edible? New Zealand's top flowers for eating are borage, these blue and white star-shaped flowers can be used in sweet or savoury dishes. The petals of calendula, commonly known as pot marigold, have a slight sweet buttery taste with a hint of pepper. Viola is a rainbow of colours! Nasturtium... Courgette... Scarlet runner... Lavender... Roses. We got to try our hand at making floral food and it was truly delightful. Most of us think of love when we send flowers - just think what may happen when we have them for dinner.

LAVENDER

Graeme and Carolyn Barrell had their first waltz together when they were just 13 years old and they danced together for over 50 years, until Graeme sadly passed away not long after we filmed their story. You may remember this couple dancing through the lavender bushes in our shows' opening titles.

The day we visited their beautiful Graelynn Lavender farm in Woodville we found them beaming with happiness and love for each other, and they proudly took us on a walk through their 10,000 lavender plants. Lynda and I, and our crew, offer Carolyn, their six children, and 27 grandchildren our heartfelt condolences.

CAROLYN'S LAVENDER ~ CHEESECAKE ~

SERVES 8-10 + PREP TIME 40 MINS + CHILLING

INGREDIENTS

Base

250g packet plain
   biscuits, crushed
100g butter, melted
Pinch of ground
   cinnamon

Topping

5 tbsp culinary
   lavender flower
   heads
¾ cup boiling water
85g packet lemon
   jelly crystals
¼ cup lemon juice
375ml chilled
   evaporated milk
250g cream cheese
¾ cup sugar
1 tsp vanilla essence

METHOD

1   To make the Base, mix biscuits, butter and cinnamon together
   and press into a 23cm springform tin. Refrigerate until firm.

2   To make the Topping, place lavender flower heads in a bowl
   with boiling water and leave to infuse for 20 minutes. Cool.
   Strain out the flower heads and reheat the infused water to
   boiling in the microwave. Dissolve jelly crystals in infused water,
   add lemon juice and set aside to cool again.

3   Beat cold evaporated milk until thick. Add cream cheese, sugar
   and vanilla and beat until lumps are removed and sugar
   dissolved. Fold through lemon/lavender infusion.

4   Pour topping over base and refrigerate for at least 3-4 hours or
   overnight if possible. Decorate before serving, if desired. Enjoy.

NOVA'S
⁎ FLOWER FRITTERS ⁎

SERVES 2 ✦ PREP TIME 10 MINS ✦ COOK TIME 10 MINS

INGREDIENTS

1 cup flour
1 tbsp caster sugar
1 cup water
1 egg white
Rice bran or coconut
   oil
Foraged edible
   flowers, prepared
   for battering
Icing sugar, to dust

METHOD

1 Whisk together flour and caster sugar in a bowl. Gradually stir in water. Press out some of the lumps of flour but there's no need to be too scrupulous. Refrigerate batter mix.

2 Beat the egg white to the soft-peak stage. Fold egg white gently into the batter mix.

3 Pour oil into pan to about 0.5cm depth. Heat until a sample blob of the batter instantly begins to brown.

4 For larger flowers, dip each flower in batter and then fry individually. With smaller flowers, mix them through the batter (preferably just before folding in the egg white), and fry dollops of mix. Some flowers, such as clover, can be pulled apart and stirred through.

5 When each fritter is golden brown, place it on a paper towel-lined plate to drain. Transfer each batch of fritters to a new plate and use a sieve to dust them generously with icing sugar.

WILD FLOWERS

When city life just gets all too hectic, taking time to stop and smell the flowers is medicine for the soul. But why stop at just a sniff when flowers taste great too?

To most it's rabbit food, but Johanna Knox has been foraging for flowers since she was a little girl and here in the middle of urban Wellington she and her daughter Nova are taking flower power to a whole new level.

FLOWERS TO USE

Elderflowers; new dandelion flowers; other DYC flowers (dandelion-like flowers); chamomile flowers; pink jasmine flowers; sweet William flowers; rose petals; clover flowers; apple blossom; pear blossom; stone fruit blossom; fennel flowers; nasturtium flowers; mustard plant flowers. Although they will add more colour than flavour you can also use borage flowers and calendula petals. Lavender, rosemary and other mint-family flowers can be used – but sparingly.

JOHANNA'S TIPS FOR PREPARING ELDERFLOWERS AND OTHER FLOWERS FOR FRITTERING

Some people like to make elderflower fritters by dunking a cluster of flowers in batter, stems still on, then frying the clusters, stem end up. To eat, you nibble the battered flowers off the stems. Other people prefer to snip the stems off while the fritters cook. However you do it, try to avoid eating or get rid of as much stem as possible. The green bits of elder are indigestible and mildly toxic (although most people seem to be able to tolerate a bit).

With other flowers, it's usual to remove stems and, if possible sepals, before battering and frying. But if you like, you certainly can leave stems on dandelion flowers, other DYCs and chamomile flowers for a 'stick' to eat them off.

Note: Dandelion flowers make particularly cute, round, juicy fritters.

TASMAN BAY ROSES

We took some time to stop and smell the roses in Motueka. Ruth Pratt is one lucky woman. She was promised a rose garden and boy did she get it! Her husband Ben has rose-growing in his blood, and here at Tasman Bay Roses they're living a life filled with love, music and more roses than you can shake a cutting at. With over 300 different varieties in their collection this garden has to be seen to be believed. Roses en masse like this make you feel giddy with joy and they taste great too.

www.tbr.co.nz

EVERYTHING SURE WAS ROSY WHEN WE VISITED BEN & RUTH PRATT IN SUNNY MOTUEKA

RUTH'S
ENGLISH ROSE CAKE

PREP TIME 1¼ HOURS + COOK TIME 40 MINS

INGREDIENTS

Crystallised Rose Petals
1 egg white
Caster sugar, to dust
Rose petals

Cake
350g butter, softened
500g golden caster sugar
6 large eggs
200g full-fat natural yoghurt
500g flour
2 tsp baking powder
1 tsp vanilla extract
1 tsp rose water

Rose Syrup
140g caster sugar
100ml water
1-2 tsp rose water, to taste

Raspberry Icing
2 tbsp Rose Syrup (see above)
85g raspberries, defrosted if frozen
250g icing sugar

Rose Cream
2 tbsp Rose Syrup (see above)
1 tsp vanilla extract
300ml double cream

To Serve
100g raspberries

METHOD

1 To make Crystallised Rose Petals, lightly whisk egg white in a small bowl. Spread caster sugar over a saucer. Holding a rose petal with tweezers, paint both sides with egg white. Spoon sugar over, then shake off the excess. Repeat with the remaining petals. Dry the petals on baking parchment for 3 hours, or overnight if possible.

2 To make the Cake, preheat oven to 160°C and grease and line the base and sides of 3 x 20cm round loose-bottomed cake tins with baking paper. Tip all the ingredients into a large bowl and beat with an electric whisk until well combined. Divide the mixture between the 3 cake tins and smooth the tops. Bake for 45 minutes, swapping the position of the tins halfway through so they cook evenly. Leave to cool for 10 minutes in the tins, then remove and transfer to a wire rack to cool completely.

3 To make the Rose Syrup, put the sugar and water in a pan and heat until the sugar has dissolved. Turn up the heat and bubble for 1-2 minutes, then remove from the heat. Add the rose water: start with 1 tsp and taste, as some varieties are much stronger than others - just be careful as the syrup will be really hot. Spoon half the syrup over the 3 sponges and set aside.

4 For the Raspberry Icing, add 2 tbsp of the syrup to the raspberries and crush them with a fork. Push the raspberries through a sieve into a bowl and discard the seeds. Sift in the icing sugar and mix to a smooth icing.

5 For the Rose Cream, add rose syrup and vanilla to cream and whisk until it holds soft peaks. Chill until needed.

6 To assemble, place one cake, flat-side up, on a plate or cake stand and top with half the Rose Cream and one-third of the raspberries. Sandwich another cake on top and add the remaining cream, another third of the raspberries, then the last cake. Smooth the Raspberry Icing over the top, letting it drizzle down the sides. Decorate with Crystallised Rose Petals and the remaining raspberries.

KEN'S
⇒ POEM ⇐

YOU USED TO GIVE THEM
TO THE MRS
TIED UP WITH BOWS AND STRINGS

AND NOW THEY TELL ME KEN
YOU CAN EAT THE BLOODY THINGS

A SALAD OF NASTURTIUMS
A CAKE WITH FLORAL ART

A LAVENDER INFUSION
AND A ROADSIDE HARVEST TART

SO HEAD OUT INTO THE MEADOW
AND GET YOURSELF A DAMN
GOOD FEED

FORGET ABOUT YOUR MEAT
AND VEG
THE NEXT BIG THING IS WEED!

KEN SMYTHE CIRCA 1975

"YA CAN'T BEAT THE SMELL OF HOT BAKED BREAD
A CLASSIC WHITE OR HEARTY GRAIN

A TURKISH BREAD - FRENCH BAGUETTE
OR A BOCADILLO LOAF FROM SPAIN

A NAAN BREAD WITH YOUR CURRY
OR FRESH BAGEL IN NEW YORK

A TASTY IRISH SODA BREAD
BAKED DOWN IN COUNTY CORK

OR THE ANCIENT SOURDOUGH FROM EUROPE
AND THE HOT JAMAICAN BAMMY

BUT YOU CAN'T BEAT THE KIWI CLASSIC
THE ICONIC MARMITE SAMMY."

- KEN MOLLER -

BREAD
⊱ WINNER ⊰

When early human beings discovered they could grind wheat and add water to make bread, life changed forever, nomadic tribes settled down, and civilisation began. This all happened about 8,000 years ago and ever since bread has been a staple food for most cultures, and has become a metaphor for life. It's amazing how many words in any language have bread in them, and are often interchangeable with money, such as "bread-winner", earning "a crust" and "dough".

Although they say man cannot live by bread alone, it's a pretty good start for many meals and we are lucky now to have access to so many different types – Turkish pita, Indian naan, Italian ciabatta, European sourdough, Māori fry bread ...the list goes on, and made from all kinds of grain. Not so long ago in Western countries bread-baking became very industrialised, and was often adulterated with toxic stuff such as chalk, so it's great to see bread being re-instated as a wholesome food. For generations, white bread was the preferred bread of the rich while the poor ate dark (wholegrain) bread. Nowadays of course it's the other way round.

We've enjoyed toast for breakfast as long as I can remember, slathered with butter and vegemite, Mum's soup just wouldn't be the same without a fresh slice of buttered bread and hard-boiled eggs are boring without the soldiers (buttered toast cut into strips) to dunk into your freshly cut egg. We are lucky in New Zealand to have a great choice of artisan breads, but there's something so nurturing about making a loaf yourself. Two of our favourite breads are challah, a Jewish bread usually baked for special occasions, introduced to us by our old friend and fellow comedian Deb Filler, and NZ's own unique Māori fry bread. Try making this at home and eating it hot with lashings of butter and jam!

SOL FILLER'S CHALLAH BREAD

The story of bread involves many twists and turns for Deb Filler and her family. From Poland and Germany to Mt Roskill, New York, Mexico and Toronto, the Filler's family history is one of adversity, survival, tremendous resilience and rising up, like the loaves of bread that NZ comedian Deb Filler's dad baked for more than 50 years. Polish-born Sol (Schaja) Filler was a much-loved and admired New Zealand citizen, as well as one of Auckland's best bakers – he introduced Aucklanders to Challah bread in the 1950s. He not only survived the unspeakable horrors of the Nazi death camps, but also kept his sense of humour intact and passed on the spirit of using that humour as a great tool for survival to his comic daughter, Deb.

We've known Deb since 1979 when we started out performing and Deb was in a band called Debbie and the Dum-dums. She left for New York City soon after then, and has performed her one-woman comi-tragedies internationally. Her 36-character show, *Punch Me in the Stomach* was based on her father's use of humour as a tool for survival and in *Filler Up!* she plays 47 characters while baking a loaf of challah bread onstage.

We feel very privileged to be gifted the Filler family's challah bread recipe, and meet Deb's lovely mum Ruth, whose German Jewish parents fled to NZ in 1938. Deb told us a funny story about her growing up in Mt Roskill in the 1960s, there were very few Jewish people there, and one day the local Presbyterian vicar, preaching to the entire school over the school intercom, informed the school it was the Jews who had killed Jesus. At the age of nine, young Debbie insisted to the vicar that her family had no part in killing Jesus and he recanted his statement publicly!

Deb Filler's combined family story is about resilience, humour, survival and sharing, because bread rises up and should be shared and that is what the Filler Family did, thanks in large part to Sol's attitude and the belief that besides love, a lack of bitterness is the best legacy. This sweet, delicious, moist bread will have you embracing the universal spirit of survival and sharing the love. You may even come back for seconds!

OUR GOOD FRIEND DEB
FILLER AND HER MUM RUTH
SHARE THEIR FAMILY'S
STORY OF SURVIVAL

FILLER FAMILY
CHALLAH BREAD

MAKES 2 LOAVES + PREP TIME 1 HOUR + RISING + COOK TIME 30-40 MINS

INGREDIENTS

3¾ tsp active dry yeast (about 1½ sachets or 11g)

1 tbsp (13g) granulated sugar

1¾ cups lukewarm water

½ cup (118 ml) vegetable oil, plus extra for greasing

3 large eggs

1 tbsp (14g) table salt

½ cup (100g) granulated sugar, extra

8-8½ cups (1000-1063g) non-bleached organic plain flour, plus extra for kneading

½ cup (about 70g) raisins per challah, plumped in hot water and drained (optional)

Poppy or sesame seeds, to sprinkle (optional)

METHOD

1 In a large bowl, dissolve yeast and sugar in water. Set aside for 5 minutes until a bit foamy.

2 Whisk oil into the yeast mixture, then beat in 2 eggs, one at a time, with salt and the extra sugar. Gradually add flour. When the dough holds together, it is ready for kneading.

3 Turn dough onto a floured surface and knead until smooth. Clean out bowl and grease it, then return dough to bowl. Cover with plastic wrap and let rise in a warm place for 1 hour, until almost doubled in size. Punch down dough, cover and let rise again in a warm place for another 30 minutes. At this point, you can knead the raisins into the challah, if you're using them, before forming the loaves.

4 To make a three-braid challah, take half the dough and form it into 3 balls. With your hands, roll each ball into a strand about 30cm long and 4cm wide. Place the 3 strands parallel to one another. Pinch the top of the strands together. Move the outside right strand over 2 strands. Then take the strand from the left and move it to the middle, like normal braid. Take the middle strand and move it over 2 strands. Continue to braid in this fashion. Make a second loaf the same way. Place the braided loaves in greased 25cm by 10cm loaf pans or on a greased cookie sheet with at least 5cm between each loaf.

5 Beat remaining egg and brush it on loaves. Either freeze the breads (remove from freezer 5 hours before baking) or leave to rise for another hour if you want to bake them immediately.

6 Preheat oven to 190°C and brush loaves with egg again. Sprinkle bread with seeds, if using.

7 Bake in the middle of your oven for 30-40 minutes, or until golden. Cool your loaves on racks - if you can wait that long. Serve with lashings of butter!

DEB'S TIPS

- The secret to good challah: Use two coats of egg wash to get that lacquer-like crust and don't overbake it. My dad used three risings which makes for the tastiest loaves, and it's even better if one of the risings is slowed down in the fridge, though not necessary. A warm moist kitchen is best.

- You can also use a mixer with a dough hook for both mixing and kneading the dough, but be careful if using a standard size mixer – it's a bit much, though it can be done.

- You can rise the dough in an oven that has been heated to 150°C and then switched off.

- Conversely, any of the three risings can be done in the fridge for a few hours, for a more deeply developed flavour. When you're ready to work with it again, it's essential to bring the dough back to room temperature before moving to the next step.

- If you have an instant read thermometer, you can take the bread out of the oven when it hits an internal temperature of 190°C.

- Use any leftovers for French toast.

- To make a 6-braided challah, take half the dough and form into 6 balls. With your hands, roll each ball into a strand tapered at the ends about 30cm long and 4cm wide. Pinch the strands together at one end, then gently spread them apart. Next, move the outside right strand over 2 strands. Then, take the second strand from the left and move it to the far right. Regroup to 3 on each side. Take the outside left strand and move it over 2 to the middle, then move the second strand from the right over to the far left. Regroup and start over with the outside right strand. Continue until all the strands are braided, tucking the ends underneath the loaf. The key is always to have 3 strands on each side, so you can keep your braid balanced. Make a second loaf the same way.

TASH'S
FRY BREAD

PREP TIME 20 MINS + RISING TIME + COOK TIME 30 MINS

INGREDIENTS

Cream Paua Filling
2 tbsp butter
1 onion, diced
6 paua, finely
    chopped
500ml cream
2 tbsp cornflour
Salt and ground black
    pepper

Dough
2.5kg high-grade flour
2 x 8g Edmonds
    Instant Dry Yeast
    sachets
1 tbsp sugar
1 tsp salt
Tepid water
1 egg, lightly beaten
Sunflower oil, to cook

METHOD

1 To make Cream Paua Filling, melt butter in a pan, add onion and
  cook for a few minutes to soften. Add paua and cream and cook
  for a couple more minutes. Add cornflour, season with salt and
  pepper and cook for 2 minutes to thicken. Set aside to cool.

2 To make the Dough, place flour, yeast, salt and sugar in bowl
  and add enough tepid water to mix to a soft dough. Knead for
  5 minutes and leave to rise for one hour.

3 Knead dough for 5 minutes and divide into equal pieces. Roll
  out each piece to 1cm thick and place some paua cream in the
  middle. Brush the edges with egg, fold over the dough and
  squish together to form a parcel around the paua filling.

4 Heat oil in a shallow pan and shallow fry the bread till brown on
  both sides.

FRY BREAD

In the Far North we visited the fry bread queen of Kaitaia, Tash Kopae. She and her gorgeous whānau are living the dream. Once they started having kids Tash and Hemi Kopae made the awesome decision to say see ya later Auckland and kia ora Ahipara. These two grew up in the far north and returned to give their children the freedom of a life that revolves around the ocean and the marae.

AHIPARA, NINETY MILE BEACH

FOR THE LOVE OF THE
BACKYARD

NO PLACE LIKE HOME

What a glorious backyard the New Zealand countryside is – from the majestic mountains in the Southern Alps to the lush native bush in the far north. We are so lucky to have access to vast national parks and public conservation land, such as Molesworth Station. But what about our own backyards, you know the little corner of the lawn with the raised beds for homegrown vegetables, or the window box in the apartment that grows all the herbs for our favourite dishes?

Our grandfather had the most amazing veggie garden at the back of his old stucco house in Mt Albert - back in the day where everyone had a quarter-acre section - he had no lawn at all, his entire backyard was full of the most amazing plants and trees. Uncle Trevor was another backyard gardener and, as well as providing for his family, he also won many first prize ribbons at the Te Kauwhata A&P Show.

How cool it would be to teach the next generation that it doesn't take too much land or effort to grow fruit and veggies for their own dinner tables.

So here's the challenge, put down the phone or the computer game and grab a shovel, some seedlings and a bag of compost and start a garden. While you're at it you may as well build your own pizza oven, and make sure the herb garden is close by to sprinkle on your homemade pizza. And remember to check the home brew in the garden shed! Why? It's fun and everything tastes good in your own backyard.

KAWHIA HARBOUR

The mighty Kawhia Harbour is Hinga and Lloyd Whiu's backyard and their whānau have looked after it for centuries. As leaders in the Māori health sector, this couple not only walk the talk but they also strut the taiaha! Inspired by her grandmother's cooking, Hinga helped re-introduce traditional Māori cooking back into their marae, including old methods of drying fish, cooking less fatty meat, and introducing more greens into meals, and this has had a positive impact on the health of not just the Whiu whānau but everyone in Kawhia. As co-organisers of Kawhia's Traditional Māori Kai Festival, which sees about 6-7000 people descend on this small town every February, Hinga and Lloyd now share their beautiful backyard with visitors from all around the world – *Lonely Planet* has placed the Kawhia Kai Festival at number three in its top 10 Māori experiences. Some of the festival's specialities are koki (shark liver pâté), kamo kamo (orange-fleshed veggies), kina, creamed paua, local oysters, whitebait fritters, toroi (mussels and puha), spit-roasted pig, fermented corn (kānga pirau) and boil-up of course!

HINGA'S PORK BONES & WATERCRESS BOIL-UP

SERVES 6-8 + PREP TIME 20 MINS + COOK TIME 1 HOUR

INGREDIENTS

5kg pork bones
About 1 tsp sea salt, or
  to taste
6 red kumara, peeled
6 potatoes, peeled
4 bunches fresh
  watercress, washed
  well

Motumotu

1 cup self-raising flour,
  plus extra to flour
  surface
A pinch of salt
Water, to mix

METHOD

1 Place pork bones in a pot with enough boiling water to cover the meat. Add sea salt. Boil pork bones for about 40 minutes or until the meat is soft. You may want to remove excess fat from the mix and replace with hot boiling water.

2 Meanwhile, make the Motumotu. Place flour and salt in a bowl with enough water to form a dough. Mix together to form a dough, knead on a floured surface then use to make little flat shapes. Set aside

3 Add potatoes and kumara to the pot with the pork bones. Break up watercress a little by twisting a bunch at a time or bruising the stalks. Add to pot. Add the motumotu and mix in with other food.

4 Boil for another 20 minutes then it's ready to eat!

HINGA'S TIP

• If the motumotu dough is too dry add water, if it's too wet add more flour.

KAWHIA, WAIKATO

HARRY'S GUINNESS CASSEROLE

PREP TIME 20 MINS + COOK TIME LONG & SLOW

INGREDIENTS

Beef for stewing (enough to make the size dish for the number that you want to feed)

Flour (enough to flour the meat)

Olive oil, for cooking

Salt and ground black pepper, to taste

Several red onions, chopped

Bay leaves

Fresh herbs such as rosemary, oregano, thyme, chopped

Bottles of Guinness (enough to cover)

½ jar home-preserved golden queen peaches

Sautéed Silverbeet

¼ cup pine nuts

1 bunch silverbeet, washed

Tarragon-flavoured oil or olive oil

Zest of 1 lime or kaffir lime

Rock salt and ground black pepper, to taste

METHOD

1 Preheat oven to 150°C.

2 Cut the beef into largish cubes and dust with flour.

3 Heat some olive oil in a casserole dish and brown the beef in batches, setting it aside in a bowl once browned.

4 Add more olive oil to the casserole dish with all the meat brownings and fry off red onion. Once the onions have softened, add bay leaves and herbs then add the browned beef back to the dish. Pour Guinness over the meat until almost totally covered with liquid, making sure that you have enough for an ale yourself.

5 Cover the dish and bake for several hours, checking occasionally to make sure that all the liquid hasn't disappeared. Halfway through the cooking add the golden queen peaches and mix through. You should end up with lovely tender meat that is coated with a very rich dark gravy.

6 When the casserole is nearly finished cooking, make the Sautéed Silverbeet. Scatter pine nuts into a clean cast iron frying pan and toast over a medium heat rolling the pine nuts by shuffling the pan across the element. Don't add any oil or fat as the pine nuts have their own oil. Watch them as they can burn quite quickly and remove from the heat when they have turned a golden brown colour. Take them out of the pan so they stop cooking and set aside to cool.

7 Slice silverbeet into strips. We remove the stalks but you could chop these finely and use these as well. Heat tarragon or plain olive oil in a large pan and cook the silverbeet until it's all wilted. Toss through the pine nuts and then sprinkle with lime zest, rock salt and pepper.

8 Serve casserole with Sautéed Silverbeet and mashed potato.

THE BACKYARD BOYS

Harry Janssen and Lloyd Houghton have been passionate about gardening for as long as they can remember. Since starting out with a roadside stall that just sold herbs 25 years ago, these green-fingered men have developed a special piece of paradise in Gordonton and their Wairere Nursery attracts people from near and far. While most of us are happy with one backyard, Harry and Lloyd have three as they keep buying properties next door but then they have a large extended family – six beloved dogs (Holly, Zac, Luca, Galaxy, Lucy and Trinity), two cats (Cigani and Magenta) along with a wide range of land and water fowl. Lloyd's Dad Pete (chief test cook) resides in a colonial cottage near the main homestead and award-winning landscape designer Anthony Skinner also lives and works at the nursery site. Harry is a passionate cook and treated us to his backyard beef stew made with homegrown vegetables.

www.wairere.co.nz

MOLESWORTH

Molesworth Station is New Zealand's biggest farm and our biggest backyard, spanning nearly half a million acres of Southern Marlborough. As it's crown land, all this beauty belongs to each and everyone of us Kiwis... and we all have a right to use it. People have lived here for over 600 years: Māori established trails for food gathering and for access between the east and west coasts. Molesworth today has an almost mythical status after recovering from devastation caused by rabbits and it's been transformed into a recreation reserve that attracts thousands of people a year. With 10,000 cattle to care for, farming legends Jim and Tracey Ward and their team have managed Molesworth for the last 15 years. We arrived for April Calf Muster. Jools joined the shepherds and Lynda hung out in the kitchen with the ladies... because we all know without them the place would fall apart! It's true what they say, behind every great man... We feel really lucky to have been invited to stay at Molesworth and meet this amazing couple.

TRACEY'S MOLESWORTH CHICKEN LASAGNE

SERVES A LARGE CROWD + PREP TIME 1½ HOURS + COOK TIME 2½ HOURS

INGREDIENTS

1 butternut pumpkin,
  peeled and chopped
  into chunks
Knob of butter
Salt and ground black
  pepper, to taste
Oil, for cooking
4-6 large onions, chopped
4-6 celery sticks, chopped
500g bacon, chopped
3 tbsp flour
3 cooked chickens, cooled,
  cooking juices reserved
  and meat shredded
500ml-1 litre chicken stock
Lasagne sheets (enough
  to cover dish with
  2 layers)
2.5 litres home-made
  cheese sauce
Silverbeet leaves (enough
  to cover dish with
  1 layer), washed
Grated cheese, to sprinkle

METHOD

1 Preheat oven to 180°C.

2 Boil pumpkin in a pot of water. When cooked, mash with
   butter and season. Set aside.

3 Heat some oil in a frying pan. Add onions, celery and bacon
   and cook. Once the onions are softened add flour. Cook for
   a minute or so then add chicken cooking juices and enough
   chicken stock to make a good sauce consistency. Add chicken
   meat to the sauce.

4 Place the chicken mixture into a large, deep dish. Cover with
   a layer of lasagne sheets. Pour about one-third of the cheese
   sauce over lasagne sheets. Lay the silverbeet on top, then
   spread over the mashed pumpkin followed by half of the
   remaining cheese sauce. Cover with another layer of lasagne
   sheets, pour remaining cheese sauce over and sprinkle some
   grated cheese on top. Bake for 1 hour.

MOLESWORTH STATION, AWATERE VALLEY

HWA851

KEN'S POEM

MOLESWORTH STATION
NO FINER PLACE ON EARTH
THERE IS NO OTHER LANDSCAPE
THAT WILL TEST A STOCKMAN'S WORTH

WHETHER RIDING FENCES
OR MARKING CALVES IN APRIL SUN
WHEN THE HORSES AND DOGS ARE FED
ONLY THEN THE DAYS WORK IS DONE

AND THE DINNER ALWAYS WELCOME
AS THE COAL RANGE FIRE GLOWS
AND UP WHERE THE CATTLE REST
IT'S THE START OF WINTER SNOWS

AND IN THE MORNING IT'S LIKE
ICING SUGAR DUSTED ON A CAKE

AND WE'RE ALL REMINDED
OF THE SMOKO COOK WILL BAKE

IT'S NOT AN EASY LAND
AT TIMES IT'S DOWN RIGHT HARD
BUT BY JEEZ, IT SURE IS
A BLOODY GOOD BACKYARD

FOR THE LOVE OF
ORGANICS

GOING GREEN

If only New Zealand had gone organic when we went nuclear free, we would have been the coolest little country in the Pacific, leading the charge on chemical-free food. Now there is such an awareness about what we eat, where it comes from and how it has been grown that a lot more people are doing the organic thing.

No harmful sprays, no toxic chemicals – but a more natural and sustainable way of farming. It may not be easy but anything worth doing takes time and a lot of commitment.

We need people who understand good animal health through good pasture management, alternative medicines such as homeopathy and the right fertilisers that don't leach nutrients from our soils. In many ways we need to return to an older way of living when the compost pile was king before the big chemical companies took charge.

I love my own organic veggie garden - I never put any spray on it - I feed it with my worm farm liquid and seaweed fertiliser. It's got about 15 tons of horse poo in it and it grows the best broccoli I've ever tasted! If you have always dreamed of having your own veggie garden, don't dilly-dally, it's easy to start with just a few pots and it's the best feeling ever watching your seedlings grow, then eating them.

ORGANIC VEGGIES

This Wairarapa Eco Farm family has a pretty cool motto – walk the talk, learn by doing and lead by example. We visited Frank van Steensel and Josje Neerincx to discover the passion behind their biodynamic market garden.

Frank and Josje both studied tropical agriculture in the Netherlands before moving out to New Zealand and in 2009 they became full-time organic farmers when they took on the Masterton orchard. They have not looked back since, enjoying the work, the community and most of all the passion that living and working with nature and healthy agriculture brings!

Wairarapa Eco Farm was initially an empty patch of land on which they planted windbreaks and olive trees, built up the soil, and designed and built an alternative green home. The farm has grown from bare paddocks into a secluded oasis. They provide fruit and veggies to over 200 families a week, wow! Everything on this farm just oozes with love.

JOSJE'S
ARTICHOKE GNOCCHI
WITH SAUTEED KALE

SERVES 4 + PREP TIME 20 MINS + COOK TIME 35 MINS

INGREDIENTS

Gnocchi
500g Jerusalem artichokes, peeled and chopped
500g floury potatoes, peeled and diced
1 large egg, lightly beaten
3-4 cups unbleached flour, plus extra for dusting
Sea salt

Sautéed Kale
2 tbsp extra virgin olive oil
¼ -½ tsp red pepper flakes
¼ tsp sea salt, plus extra
Ground black pepper to taste
1 large onion, chopped
4 cloves garlic, finely chopped
1 large bunch of kale, washed and cut into ribbons
2 tbsp white wine vinegar
1 tbsp lemon zest

To Serve
¼ cup shaved parmesan cheese
Olive oil, to drizzle

METHOD

1 Boil Jerusalem artichoke and potato in a large pot of cold water for 20-25 minutes, or until easily mashed with a fork. Drain and, when cool enough to handle, push them through a ricer or mash with a fork.

2 Set the riced mixture on a lightly floured work surface, make a well, and place egg in the middle. Sprinkle flour over, 1 cup at a time, adding up to 3 cups. Use a pastry scraper to fold the flour into the mixture (the mixture will be fairly sticky). With a light touch, continue adding the remaining cup of flour, or just enough so that the dough stops sticking to your fingers. Once the dough is holding together, knead it lightly for a minute or so. Form into an oblong mound, and then use the pastry scraper or a knife to divide into 8 sections.

3 On a well-floured work surface, gently roll each section into a long, 32cm tube. Use a sharp knife to cut off 1cm sections, make an indentation in the centre with your fingertip, and set on a lightly floured tray.

4 Bring a large stockpot of water to a rapid boil. Add enough sea salt that a drop of the water tastes like the sea. Gently lower several gnocchi at a time into the water and as soon as they float back to the top, remove from water with a slotted spoon and set aside. Drizzle cooked gnocchi with a bit of olive oil.

5 Meanwhile, make the Sautéed Kale. Heat a large skillet over a medium-high heat. Heat extra virgin olive oil until shimmery, add red pepper flakes, sea salt and black pepper. Add onions, and sauté until translucent. Add garlic and sauté for a further minute. Add the kale, a little at a time, along with a pinch of sea salt for each batch. Cook until kale has wilted down. Sprinkle in the vinegar and lemon zest. Turn heat to low, and cook for another 5 minutes or so.

6 Spoon Sautéed Kale over a handful of gnocchi and finish with the shaved parmesan and a drizzle of olive oil.

JILL'S
SEAWEED &
❧ CARROT LOAF ❧

MAKES 1 LOAF + PREP TIME 10 MINS + COOK TIME 35 MINS

INGREDIENTS

250g flour
1½ tbsp baking
   powder
110g butter, melted
4 eggs
125g Ecklonia radiata
   (Seaweed), finely
   chopped
1 large carrot, peeled
   and grated
Cream cheese, to
   serve (optional)

METHOD

1 Preheat oven to 180°C. Grease and line a 7cm x 13cm x 23cm loaf
   tin.

2 Sift flour and baking powder into a bowl.

3 In another bowl, beat together melted butter and egg until
   combined.

4 Gradually add flour mixture to butter mixture and mix well with
   spatula. Fold in carrot and seaweed.

5 Pour into the loaf tin and bake for 35-40 minutes, or until a knife
   inserted into the centre comes out clean. Allow to cool in the tin
   for a few minutes then transfer to a wire rack to cool completely.

6 Slice and serve with cream cheese or your choice of savoury
   toppings.

ORGANIC SEAWEED

Keith Atwood and Jill Bradley are fertiliser pioneers of the seaweed variety. Founders of AgriSea, a certified organic company based in Paeroa, they are changing the way New Zealand farmers increase their productivity by applying seaweed nutritional product to the land. But the seaweed's not just destined for agriculture, they eat it and drink it too.

Jill and Keith were qualified teachers working with at-risk students in Auckland when they decided to "see our country" in the early 90s by labouring for free on the land. They took part in WWOOFing on a series of organic farms, before working on one that used seaweed as its major input. The food tasted so good, how they remembered it from childhood. They decided to take a punt, "hold hands and jump off a cliff", by putting everything they had into it. And now almost 20 years later, AgriSea employs more than 30 staff, has four factories and contracts dozens of families living near remote beaches of the east coast of the North Island to gather beachcast brown seaweed for its products.

Seaweed is saving the earth – it's the way of the future! "Organic" is becoming mainstream thanks a lot to Jill and Keith, and their adult kids Tane and Clare, who also run the company. AgriSea continues to spend a small fortune on researching the benefits of seaweed use and diversifying their products. While the Japanese have understood the health benefits of seaweed for years, Kiwis have been slow to make the most of harvesting our coastal plants. Our native species *Ecklonia radiata*, is one of the most complex materials in the world, full of excellent nutrition. You can try it in Jill's special loaf recipe.

www.agrisea.co.nz

ORGANIC DAIRY

We're back in the milking shed! It's been 30 long years but we haven't lost our touch. You can't beat a teat!
Janette and Neil Perrett have been milking cows all their lives - they grew up in dairy families, met on a farm,
and now farm organically with their daughter Carla and her son, Ethan. It's a real family affair but with Neil
semi-retired and taking a back seat, it's the girls that run this show! They move their herd of 150 organic dairy
cows to wherever the grass is greenest. The cows and humans alike are living the organic dream.

THE PERRETT'S
ORGANIC SILEAGE WAS
EVEN GOOD ENOUGH
FOR LYNDA TO EAT!

⸙ ORGANIC KEFIR ⸙

INGREDIENTS

About 1 tbsp kefir
  grains (see Tip)
1 litre fresh organic
  milk

METHOD

1 Place kefir grains in an Agee jar (or similar) and fill jar with organic milk.

2 Leave the jar on the kitchen bench, covered to keep out insects but loose enough to allow the kefir to breathe (muslin cloth works well).

3 After about 24 hours your kefir will be ready to strain through a non-metal colander or similar.

4 Once drained, the granules can be placed into a clean jar with a new supply of milk.

JANETTE'S TIPS

- The best way to obtain the kefir granules is from other people so ask around.

- The longer the culture stands on the bench the tarter it can become. Some people like it that way - the choice is yours.

- The nicest batch is made with pure organic cream - absolutely amazing flavour but again the longer it stands the tarter it will become. If this happens simply strain the granules and start again. They are very forgiving.

- In time you will see multiplication occurring - a real miracle! (They do slow in the winter months.)

Kefir is basically fermented milk, it tastes like a drinkable yoghurt. It contains high levels of vitamin B12, calcium, magnesium, vitamin K2, biotin, folate, enzymes and probiotics. It's made with kefir "grains", a yeast/bacterial fermentation starter.

LAKE MATHESON, AORAKI, MT COOK

KEN'S
⊰ POEM ⊱

NEW ZEALAND LET'S GET CRACKING
IT'S TIME TO GO ORGANIC

IF WE ALL PULLED TOGETHER
WE COULD SAVE THIS BLOODY PLANET

NO CHEMICALS OR PESTICIDES
WE'D ALL BE PLEASED AS PUNCH

COS THERE'S NOTHING MORE
REVOLTING
THAN POISON IN YOUR LUNCH

THE TIMES THEY ARE CHANGING,
WE'D BE PROUD OF WHAT WE SELL

COS THE PRODUCT THAT YOU'RE
MAKING
WOULD BE OH SO NATURAL

FOR THE LOVE OF
THE BUSH

GOING BUSH

Love of the bush and being in it, is part of our Kiwi identity. New Zealand's native bush vegetation is so benign on one hand, no poisonous snakes or insects threaten your enjoyment factor, but every year people get injured or lose their way in the New Zealand bush. Not many of us could survive out in it for too long, even overnight. So whether it's a day tramp or a longer adventure, it's important to be prepared and take enough food and water, rain gear, warm clothes, a phone or beacon, and let people know where you are going. Perhaps, with all the natural disasters happening around the world and change on the increase, we should be thinking about our survival skills? We learnt about survival in the NZ Army when we were young, and then taught young people bush survival skills when we lived at Te Henga, West Auckland, in the early 80s. Our city-dwelling friends often joke that in the event of an emergency they will just hitch a ride to one of our places, but really we urge everyone to get a survival kit together, and mentally rehearse what you'd do in the event of "the big one". Just like a good cook - it helps to be prepared!

Close to Jools' home, the Waitakere Ranges are Auckland's crown jewel. Millions of hectares of native bush right on our doorstep. But kauri die-back is a big threat to our majestic iconic trees. We got to hang out with one of the Waitakeres' Park Rangers whose job it is to protect this taonga for future generations, and want to pass on his message of kaitiaki - remember we are only guardians of this beautiful land we live in.

BUSH FOOD

Michelle has worked with us for 10 years. Her husband, Jason Duff (Te Whānau-ā-Apanui, Ngāi Tahu), is a park ranger for the Auckland Council in the Waitakere Ranges, and they are lucky to live right in the middle of them. When Michelle told us they have native crayfish (koura) in their stream we didn't believe her, so she invited us out for lunch. Jason laid down a wild pork hangi seasoned with horopito and kawakawa and Michelle showed us how to make her pikopiko (fern frond) salad. Simply the most delicious bush tucker we've ever eaten. Wild freshwater koura are protected and their existence in the Waitakere Ranges is at risk with their numbers sadly declining. While they are a tough, long-lived species they are sensitive to pollutants, herbicides and insecticides. So, we ate koura sourced from a freshwater crayfish farm in the South Island. We take our hats off to the park rangers and conservationists who are working hard to preserve and protect Auckland's huge backyard.

THE DUFF WHANAU
JASON & MICHELLE WITH
THEIR GORGEOUS KIDS
MARY, TOBY & JOHN.

MICHELLE'S
KOURA WITH
~ PIKOPIKO ~

SERVES 4 + PREP TIME 10 MINS + COOK TIME 5 MINS

INGREDIENTS

200g pikopiko heads/
    spears
1kg cooked
    freshwater koura
    tails
2-3 mandarins, peeled
    and segmented
¼ cup good-quality
    olive oil
Juice of 2-3 mandarins
Salt and ground black
    pepper, to taste

METHOD

1 Carefully wash the pikopiko tips in cold water and use your
   fingers to rub off the brown speckles along the stalk. Also remove
   the small fern-shaped leaves.

2 Lightly steam for a few minutes until bright green as you would
   asparagus. Don't overcook or they will loose their lovely crunch.

3 Lay the pikopiko on a serving plate and place the koura tails and
   mandarin around.

4 Mix olive oil and mandarin juice and season with salt and pepper
   to taste to make a dressing. Drizzle the dressing over over the
   dish and serve.

MAUREEN'S
ASIAN BARBECUE
⋇ TROUT ⋇

SERVES 4 ＋ PREP TIME 5 MINS ＋ COOK TIME 12 MINS

INGREDIENTS

Whole fresh trout,
  cleaned and gutted
1 bunch of fresh
  coriander
2-3 sprigs fresh mint
Smoked garlic salt
Pinch of chilli powder
1 tsp dried mixed
  herbs

METHOD

1 Score the skin of the trout and stuff with fresh herbs.

2 Rub the outside of the trout with smoked garlic salt and chilli
   powder and sprinkle with dried mixed herbs.

3 Place trout in stainless steel barbecue fish grilling basket and
   place over hot barbecue until cooked through – about 12
   minutes.

HURUNUI JACKS LUXURY GLAMPING

Once upon a time, Maureen Spencer and John Plows were high-flying fashionistas, who shared a professional relationship before falling in love later in life. John started the iconic Kiwi clothing label Global Culture and travelled the world making the brand a huge success. But then he decided to follow his dreams, and left the high-pressure world of the fashion industry behind. Together he and Maureen, who originally hails from Yorkshire, created Hurunui Jacks, a glamping and outdoor experience, deep in the heart of the Hokitika bush. A wonderland where ancient native bush rolls down to the river with trout leaping literally on the doorstep! Hurunui is the name of John's favourite hunting/fishing grounds, the Hurunui River in Canterbury. Since we met them, John has sadly passed away. His story is a reminder to us all to live our dreams and follow your heart. Maureen, we are so sorry for your loss. Thanks for the wonderful hospitality you showed us that magical day. Trout has never tasted so good.

www.hurunuijacks.co.nz

RIP JOHN PLOWS
A BLOODY GREAT
PARTNER, FISHERMAN &
LOVER OF LIFE

HURUNUI JACKS
WELCOMES

LYNDA

JOOLS

THE KIWI BUSHMAN

Move over Bear Grylls, here comes Josh the Kiwi Bushman also known as the "Possum whisperer". Josh Marcotte is a true West Coaster, YouTube sensation and now TV star. Hunter, fisherman, possum plucker, white water rafter – this man is an expert in survival skills and an archetypal male, who respects nature instead of exploiting it. The day we visited he'd just got back from around the world filming a new survival show, *Kings of the Wild,* for the Discovery Channel. They signed him up after his videos, shot with a GoPro camera, became an internet success, recording up to 40,000 hits a week on his YouTube channel. And beside every bushman there is an outstanding woman – his Canadian wife, Kristen, keeps the home fires burning, the bubbles bubbling and the babies fed. This family are living a truly sustainable life most of us could only dream of - Josh hunts or catches most of their food, Kristen's vegetable garden is bountiful, and their three boys are growing up immersed in nature. We shared a special day with this remarkable family and ate heartily from Mother Nature's bounty. Our director Felicity Morgan-Rhind is an amazing chef, she trained with Peter Gordon in London before she became a film-maker, and we reckon her Feijoa salsa (see opposite) is the best – especially with seared venison.

www.thekiwibushman.co.nz

FELICITY'S
⁂ FEIJOA SALSA ⁂
FOR WILD GAME MEAT

SERVES 4-6 + PREP TIME 10 MINS + REST TIME

INGREDIENTS

20 feijoas, flesh
  scooped out and
  roughly chopped
2 cloves garlic,
  crushed
½ cup thinly sliced red
  onion
A handful of chopped
  parsley
½ tsp salt
Ground black pepper,
  to taste
2 tbsp olive oil
3 tbsp crumbled feta
  (optional)

METHOD

1 Place all ingredients except feta, if using, in a bowl and mix to
   combine. Set aside to rest for 30 minutes. Add crumbled feta
   just before serving with your favourite wild pork or venison.

KEN'S BUSH POEM

WHEN I WAS JUST A LITTLE BOY
MY DADDY SAT ME ON HIS KNEE

YOU CAN'T BEAT THE
GREAT OUTDOORS
IS WHAT HE SAID TO ME

THE BUSH IS A GLORIOUS PLACE
FULL OF BERRIES, ANIMALS AND SEEDS

IT'S A BUSHMAN'S PANTRY
IT'S A SMORGASBORD
OF EVERYTHING HE NEEDS

SO HEAD UP INTO THE BUSH-CLAD
HILLS
NO FINER PLACE TO ROAM

COOK UP A BREW IN THE OLD TIN HUT
IT'S OUR HOME AWAY FROM HOME

FOR THE LOVE OF
DECADENCE

INDULGE ❧ YOURSELF ❧

Many foods conjure up a great sense of emotion for many people and words and phrases such as desirable, satisfying, self-indulgent, sinfully good, a bit naughty and decadent are often used to describe food experiences that are so exceptional and indulgent. Decadence is defined as something that is "characterised by or reflecting a state of moral or cultural decline" or "luxuriously self-indulgent". So foods that are described as "decadent" are those that people feel the taste too good to be morally sound.

Of course this is silly. Pleasure has often been linked with moral decline, thanks to religion, when actually it's simply experiencing joy.

Everyone's favourite indulgence is unique to them, whether it's rich desserts or expensive foods such as truffles, crayfish and Champagne, or a lie-in on a Saturday morning with a hot crumpet and a cup of tea. For us, chocolate is probably one of the most decadent foods around – we crave it, savour it and morally beat ourselves up a bit for having too much. Chocolate mousse, hand-made chocolate truffles, chocolate biscuits, chocolate cake, hot chocolate with marshmallows, mmmm. We are hardly morally corrupt for reaching out for that extra piece of creamy cocoa confectionary though. It makes us feel euphoric just for that instant – the moment it melts in our mouths – a pleasurable second or two.

So let's drop the guilt. Go on be a little decadent, as long as it's not damaging your health, but like mama says, "Nothing in excess".

OAKLAND TRUFFIERE

Alan and Lynley Hall were the first to grow truffles in New Zealand and the first truffière in the Southern Hemisphere to produce the Périgord black truffle (*Tuber melanosporum*) – a delicacy desired around the world for its pungent and aromatic taste, nicknamed "Black Diamond" due to its mouth-watering price tag – it can sell for as much as $3500 per kg! They took us hunting with their truffle-hunting dog Marco, an Italian breed called Lagotto, specially trained to find truffles. And Marco did not disappoint!

LYNLEY'S
BBQ CHICKEN
⇒ WITH TRUFFLES ⇒

SERVES 4 + PREP TIME 1 HOUR + COOK TIME 30 MINS

INGREDIENTS

4 skin-on chicken breasts
1 fresh truffle, finely shaved
8 rashers streaky bacon
¼ tsp flaky sea salt
¼ tsp ground black pepper
1 tbsp olive oil
Salad, to serve

METHOD

1 Preheat oven 180°C.

2 Make an incision into the thicker part of each chicken breast with a knife, creating a small pocket. Stuff shaved truffle into the pocket of each breast. Wrap each breast with 2 rashers then season with salt and pepper.

3 Heat olive oil in a medium frying pan over a high heat. Once the oil begins to smoke, add the chicken breasts skin-side down and cook for 3 minutes. Turn and cook or another 3 minutes. They should be golden brown on each side.

4 Transfer the chicken breasts to an oven roasting dish and cook in the for 20-25 minutes until cooked through. Serve with a salad on the side.

LYNLEY'S TIP

● If you don't have a fresh truffle available to you, you can get a jar of sliced summer truffles, available at Sabato.

CHRIS'S CRAYFISH WITH ⇒ LIME OIL ⇒

SERVES 4 + PREP TIME 10 MINS + COOK TIME 8 MINS

INGREDIENTS

2 crayfish
¼ cup avocado lime oil
Salt ground black pepper, to taste

METHOD

1 Bring a large pot of sea water to the boil. When boiling add crayfish and cook for 8 minutes. Remove crayfish from pot and leave to cool for 5 minutes or so.

2 Cut crayfish down the middle from head to tail. Lay them on a platter. Drizzle with avocado lime oil and season with salt and pepper.

HOW TO HUMANELY AND CORRECTLY KILL AND COOK CRAYFISH

The only humane way to kill a crayfish is to chill it at between 2°C and 4°C until it is "insensible" and safely immobile. It can then be killed with a sharp instrument either by head spiking (between the eyes) or chest spiking (through the chest wall from the underside).

CRAYFISH.

A tropical storm was blowing when we visited Dive Tatapouri just north of Gisborne but that never stops Chris and Dean Savage from playing in the paradise they have created here. Situated right on the Wainui beach, they offer unforgettable reef tours amongst wild stingrays.

Dean is a qualified diver and skipper with more than 40 years' commercial diving experience and has also been an underwater cameraman for New Zealand's *Tangaroa with Pio* TV show and has filmed in exotic locations all over New Zealand, the Pacific and Chile. Chris is a born and bred Gisborne girl and we must say Gisborne hospitality is amongst the best we have ever experienced. Freshly caught crayfish on the fire, with Chris' special lime oil and a fresh salad, all washed down with a cold beer and local white wine – no wonder this place is one of NZ's most popular tourist attractions.

www.divetatapouri.com

CHOCOLATE

Edith Mueller and Pascal Sigrist met on a Latino dance floor in Switzerland. Twenty years later we found them making the most delectable Swiss chocolate in Waitoki, west of Auckland, and they're still dancing, even though Pascal sadly became paraplegic after a car accident. But this positive-minded guy does not let this injury limit his life. He still sails a small boat solo and runs Swiss Bliss with his wife. You could say Lynda and I are chocolate connoisseurs, we love hand-made high-cocoa chocolate. We certainly think Edith and Pascal's business is well-named. *www.swissbliss.nz*

DID YOU KNOW?

- The cacao trees' scientific name *Theobroma cacao* literally translates to 'cacao, food of the Gods'.
- Dark chocolate is actually loaded with minerals and one of the best sources of antioxidants on the planet.
- The smell of chocolate increases theta brain waves, which triggers relaxation.
- Chocolate gives you a more intense mental high and gets your heart pounding more than kissing does.
- Hot chocolate used to be believed to be an aphrodisiac.
- Eating dark chocolate every day can reduce your chance of heart disease by one-third.
- Chocolate can be lethal to dogs so don't leave your chocolate lying around for your pooch to devour.

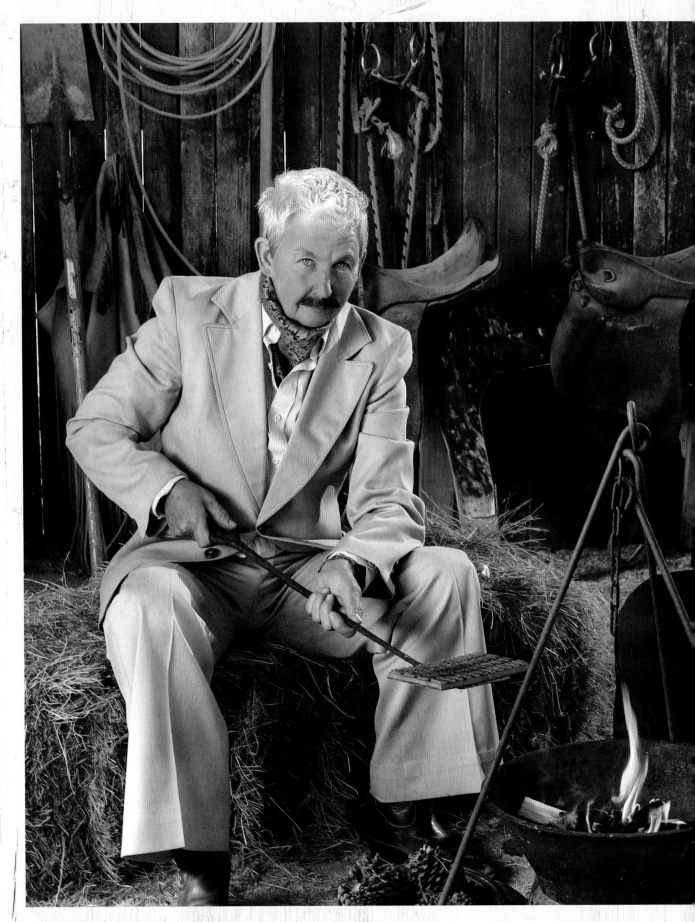

KEN'S DECADENCE POEM

LAY BACK IN YOUR VELVET CHAIR
WITH YOUR SLIPPERS AND YOUR PIPE

THE PORT HAS BEEN DECANTED
AND THE CHEESE IS PERFECTLY RIPE

WE'LL STOKE UP THE FIRE
ON A COLD WINTER'S NIGHT

AND WE'LL HAVE A SMIDGE OF
CAVIAR
JUST A LITTLE BITE

WHILE YOU'RE AT IT PASS THE OLIVES
AND THE CHOCOLATE IF YOU PLEASE

AND WE'LL TOP IT OFF WITH BRANDY
AND A PLATE OF BLUE VEIN CHEESE

IS THERE ANY PRAWN MORNAY?
OR A MANLY IRISH STOUT?

AND WE'LL FINISH OF MY FRIEND WITH
A LITTLE DASH OF GOUT...

MARVELLOUS!

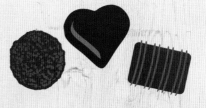

TASTY
TREATS
WITH THE
BOWLING LADIES

GOATS' CHEESE, SAUSAGE & PINEAPPLE SKEWERS

INGREDIENTS
3 good-quality pork
  sausages
8 cubes goats' cheese
8 cubes fresh
  pineapple
¼ cup warm honey

METHOD

1 Preheat barbecue to medium.

2 Grill sausages about 5 minutes per side. Cut into 8 chunks.

3 Thread in the following order on each toothpick sausage chunk, cheese cube, and pineapple cube.

4 Drizzle with warm honey and serve.

CURRIED EGGS

INGREDIENTS
6 free range eggs
¼ tsp salt
1 tsp mild curry
  powder
¼ cup fresh curly
  parsley, finely
  chopped
Salt and ground black
  pepper, to taste

Mayonnaise
2 free-range eggs
2 cloves garlic, finely
  chopped
Zest and juice of
  1 lemon
1 tbsp white vinegar
1 tsp salt
1 tsp ground black
  pepper
400ml vegetable oil

METHOD

1 Bring a medium pot of cold water to the boil. Add eggs and boil for 10 minutes.

2 While the eggs are boiling, make the Mayonnaise. Place eggs, garlic, lemon zest and juice, vinegar, salt and pepper in the bowl of a food processor. With the motor running, slowly drizzle in the oil until the mixture starts to thicken and emulsify. Place ½ cup in a bowl and chill the leftovers in a covered jar.

3 Remove eggs from heat and cool under cold water. Peel under running water and carefully cut the eggs in half lengthways. Gently pop out the yolks and place in a medium bowl. Set aside the whites.

4 Mash the yolks lightly with a fork, add the curry powder, parsley, salt and pepper and reserved ½ cup mayonnaise. Mix to combine and place in a piping bag.

5 Pipe the curried egg mixture back onto the egg whites. Garnish with extra ground black pepper.

JELLIED PINEAPPLE

INGREDIENTS
425g can sliced
   pineapple, drained
   and juice reserved
85g packet of lime
   jelly

METHOD

1 In a bowl dissolve jelly in ½ cup boiling water. Add the reserved pineapple juice and stir. Pour jelly mix into can over pineapple slices and refrigerate until set.

2 When jelly is set, run a little hot water over sides and bottom of can to loosen. Then cut bottom from can and use to push mold out. Cut between pineapple slices and serve.

SCOTCH EGGS

INGREDIENTS
125g flour, plus extra
   to flour surface
Salt and ground
   black pepper
1 egg, beaten
180g dry
   breadcrumbs
300g good-quality
   sausage meat
50g Greek-style
   natural yoghurt
4 large eggs (free
   range), hardboiled
   and peeled
Vegetable oil, to
   deep fry
Salt and ground
   black pepper

Dipping Sauce:
150g Greek-style
   natural yoghurt
2 tbsp wholegrain
   mustard

METHOD

1 Place the flour in one plate or dish and season with salt and pepper. Place the beaten egg in another plate or dish and the breadcrumbs in a third plate or dish.

2 Mix the sausage meat with the yoghurt in a bowl and season. Divide the meat mixture into 4 balls and flatten each out on a clean floured surface.

3 Dredge each egg in the seasoned flour. Place one round of sausage meat over each egg and wrap around so the whole egg is covered, making sure the coating is as smooth as possible.

4 Dip each coated egg into the beaten egg and then roll into the breadcrumbs until you have a complete covering.

5 Heat the vegetable oil in a deep heavy bottomed pan. The oil is hot enough when a breadcrumb sizzles when it is dropped in.

6 Using a slotted spoon, carefully place each egg into the hot oil and deep-fry for 10 minutes until golden. Move the eggs around with the spoon so they cook evenly. Remove each egg from the oil and drain on kitchen paper.

7 Mix together the yoghurt and the mustard until both are incorporated and serve in a dish alongside the scotch eggs.

BOWLING LADIES' TIPS

• You can use sausages in the skin, just remove the meat from the skin.

• Flour your hands before wrapping the eggs in sausage meat.

SPREADS ON BREAD

INGREDIENTS

Green Topping
½ loaf wholemeal
   bread
250g cottage cheese
½ cup fresh parsley,
   finely chopped
1 spring onion, finely
   chopped
Zest and juice of
   1 lemon
¼ tsp salt
¼ tsp black pepper
350g jar cornichons
   (French-style baby
   gherkins)

METHOD

1 Remove crusts and roll out bread slices using a rolling pin to slightly compact, then cut into small shapes using cookie cutters or into simple squares or triangles by hand.

2 Place cottage cheese, parsley, spring onion, lemon zest and juice, salt and pepper in a medium bowl and mix to combine.

3 Spread onto bread and garnish with a cornichon.

Other topping ideas: *(see image previous page)*

Red – Sour cream and beetroot decorated with orange segments and cucumber.

White – Cream cheese and lemon decorated with slices of salami and stuffed olives.

BANGERS IN CAULIFLOWER

INGREDIENTS

(8 to 10) Sausages
1 free range egg,
   beaten
½ cup cornflake
   crumbs
½ cup Flour
1 large raw cauliflower

METHOD

1 Pre heat oven to 180°C.

2 Score surface of Sausages lightly, spiralling from end to end.

3 Insert wood skewers in one end. Roll each sausage in flour then beaten egg, and roll in cornflake crumbs.

4 Line an oven tray with baking paper. Place sausages in pan; do not crowd.

5 Bake in oven for about 15 minutes.

6 Poke skewers into raw cauli and ensure wobble dramatically when serving to guests. Serve with home-made tomato relish or with mustard, if desired.

GOLDEN JUBILEE GINGER LOG

INGREDIENTS

300ml cream
1 tsp vanilla essence
1 tbsp icing sugar
About 1 cup
   "dunking" liquid of
   your choice e.g.
   orange juice, sherry,
   brandy, lemonade,
   ginger ale
300g packet
   gingernut biscuits

To Serve

Grated chocolate, to
   sprinkle or
   chocolate or
   caramel sauce, to
   drizzle

METHOD

1 Place cream in a large stainless steel mixing bowl. Beat with electric beaters or a food mixer on a slow setting and gently increase the speed. Once the cream begins to leave a trail after the beaters add the vanilla essence and icing sugar and continue to mix on a medium speed until soft peaks form. Mix for a few seconds more until you have stiff peaks and set aside.

2 Place "dunking" liquid of your choice in a shallow bowl. Choose a serving plate, ensuring it is long enough to hold the packet of biscuits with a few centimetres spare either end. Smear some whipped cream across the plate to form a base to hold the biscuits.

3 Take the first biscuit and dunk it briefly, then smear one side with cream and place it vertically on the plate - the first one may fall but the next biscuit will hold it up. Take the second biscuit, dunk it briefly in the liquid, smear one side with cream and place it up against the first biscuit. Repeat until all the biscuits are used up and form a straight line.

4 Take the remaining cream and gently smear all over the top and sides of the log of biscuits, smoothing as best you can. Chill the cream-covered log for at least 6 hours, and preferably overnight, to allow the biscuits to soften before serving.

5 Serve covered with a sauce or grated chocolate.

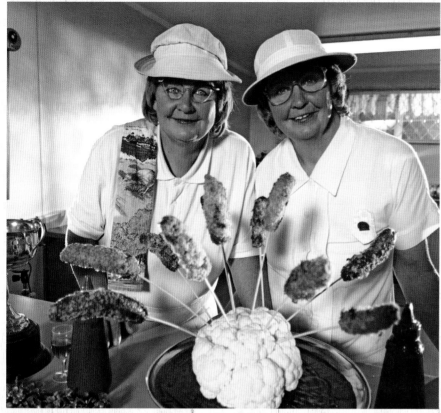

ᵕ RECIPE INDEX ᵕ

A

Anna's Brine Pork Roast 26
Annie's Duck Curry 111
Apples
 Apple Sauce 134
 Grandma Hora's Apple Shortcake 121
 Phil's Mum's Stuffed Turkey 109
Artichokes, Josje's Artichoke
Gnocchi with Sautéed Kale 221
Avocado
 Avocado Salsa 47
 Wild Salad 53

B

Bacon
 Lynda's Duck Breast Paté 130
 Nana's Bacon Balls 18
Baking see also Desserts; Pastry
 Jill's Seaweed & Carrot Loaf 222
 Nana's Gingernut Biscuits 126
 Ruth's English Rose Cake 191
Bangers in Cauliflower 254
Barbecue
 Belinda's Roast Angus with
  Smoked Garlic 99
 Frank's Crab Apple Salmon with
  Kelp Chips 53
 Jeremy's Salmon and Salsa Burgers 47
 Lynley's Barbecue Chicken with
  Truffles 241
 Maureen's Asian Barbecue Trout 232
 Tim's Barbecued Backstrap with
  Brandy Sauce 59
Beef
 Belinda's Roast Angus with
  Smoked Garlic 99
 Dan Dan Sauce 177
 Freddy's Dan Dan Noodles 177
 Harry's Guinness Casserole 210
 Jason's Butcher's Pie 100
Beetroot, Sunny's Beetroot &
Fennel Soup 71
Belinda's Roast Angus with
Smoked Garlic 99
Biscuits see Baking
Blackberries, Pear & Blackberry
Sauce 138
Blueberries, Carolann's Blueberry
Buttermilk Pancakes 154
Blue cheese
 Janet's Blue Cheesy Mushrooms 42
 Lynda's Duck Breast Paté 130
Boil-up, Hinga's Pork Bones &
Watercress Boil-Up 208
Brandy Sauce 59
Bread dishes see also Burgers
 Filler Family Challah Bread 198
 Naan Bread 62
 Phil's Mum's Stuffed Turkey 109
 Spreads on Bread 253
 Tash's Fry Bread 200
Bridgette's Pheasant Pies 119

Bruce's Cold Smoked Salmon 48
Buffalo Mozzarella Gratin 165
Burgers
 Jeremy's Salmon and Salsa Burgers 47
 Rosemary's Ostrich Steak &
  Egg Burgers 163
Buttermilk, Carolann's Blueberry
Buttermilk Pancakes 154

C

Cakes see Baking
Capers, Creamy Caper & Gherkin
Sauce 138
Carolann's Blueberry Buttermilk
Pancakes 154
Carolyn's Lavender Cheesecake 187
Carrots
Jason's Butcher's Pie 100
Jill's Seaweed and Carrot Loaf 222
Casserole, Harry's Guinness Casserole 210
Cauliflower, Bangers in Cauliflower 254
Challah see Bread dishes
Cheese see also specific cheeses
 Carolyn's Lavender Cheesecake 187
 Cheese Fondue 136
 Jason's Butcher's Pie 100
 Nana's Bacon Balls 18
Chicken
 Lynley's Barbecue Chicken with
  Truffles 241
 Tracey's Molesworth Chicken
  Lasagne 213
Chilli
 Avocado Salsa 47
 Green Chilli Sauce 136
 Libby's Delhi Dahl 173
 Tanah's La You Chilli Oil 174
 Three Little Birds' Curry Goat 146
Chips, Kelp Chips 53
Chorizo
 Janice's Seafood & Saffron Paella 91
 Mariano's Ous Al Plat 23
Chris' Crayfish with Lime Oil 242
Cockles
 Fleur's Cod & Cockles in a Kelp Bag 80
 John's Mashpee Indian Clambake 86
Coconut, Whipped Coconut Cream 136
Cod, Fleur's Cod & Cockles in a
 Kelp Bag 80
Cointreau Drizzle 148
Corn
 John's Mashpee Indian Clambake 86
 Jools' One Egg Corn Fritters 129
Crayfish
 Chris' Crayfish with Lime Oil 242
 Michelle's Koura with Pikopiko 231
Cream, flavoured see Toppings
Cream Paua Filling 200
Creamy Caper & Gherkin Sauce 138
Crystallised Rose Petals 191
Cucumber, Tzatziki 134
Curried Eggs 250

Curries
 Annie's Duck Curry 111
 Curried Eggs 250
 Marg's Rump Curry with
  Naan Bread 62
 Three Little Birds' Curry Goat 146

D

Dahl, Libby's Delhi Dahl 173
Damsons, Heather's Damson Paste 153
Dan Dan Sauce 177
Daphne's Mum's Mum's Honey Steamed
Pudding 122
Dates, Daphne's Mum's Mum's Honey
Steamed Pudding 122
Desserts see also Baking
 Carolyn's Lavender Cheesecake 187
 Daphne's Mum's Mum's Honey
  Steamed Pudding 122
 Golden Jubilee Ginger Log 254
 Grandma Hora's Apple Shortcake 121
 Jo's Feijoa Self-Saucing Pudding 157
Dips see Sauces
Drinks
 Golden Turmeric Latte 181
 Organic Kefir 225
Drizzles see Sauces, sweet
Duck
 Annie's Duck Curry 111
 Duck Stock 111
 Lynda's Duck Breast Paté 130

E

Eggs
 Creamy Caper & Gherkin Sauce 138
 Curried Eggs 250
 Jools' One Egg Corn Fritters 129
 Julie's Kelmarna Waiata Frittata 75
 Mariano's Ous Al Plat 23
 Nova's Flower Fritters 188
 Rosemary's Ostrich Steak and
  Egg Burgers 163
 Scotch Eggs 252
 Spicy Hollandaise Sauce 134

F

Feijoas
 Felicity's Feijoa Salsa for Wild Game
  Meat 235
 Jo's Feijoa Self-Saucing Pudding 157
Fennel
 Fleur's Cod & Cockles in a Kelp Bag 80
 Sunny's Beetroot & Fennel Soup 71
Figs
 Helen's Fig & Goats' Cheese Tart 72
 Pam's Roast Goat with Figs &
  Herbs 143
Filler Family Challah Bread 198
Fillings, Cream Paua Filling 200

Fiona's Fried Grasshoppers with
 Satay Sauce 167

Fish see also specific fish,
Janice's Seafood & Saffron Paella   91
Fleur's Cod & Cockles in a Kelp Bag   80
Flowers see also specific flowers,
Nova's Flower Fritters   188
Fondues see Sauces
Frank's Crab Apple Salmon with
   Kelp Chips   53
Freddy's Dan Dan Noodles   177
Frittata, Julie's Kelmarna Waiata
   Frittata   75
Fritters
   Jools' One Egg Corn Fritters   129
   Nova's Flower Fritters   188

G
Galangal, Mac's Turmeric Tarakihi   180
Garlic
   Belinda's Roast Angus with
     Smoked Garlic   99
   Infused Oil   59
   Sautéed Kale   221
Gherkins, Creamy Caper & Gherkin
   Sauce   138
Ginger
   Apple Sauce   134
   Golden Jubilee Ginger Log   254
   Golden Turmeric Latte   181
   Nana's Gingernut Biscuits   126
   Peanut Sauce   136
Gnocchi, Josje's Artichoke Gnocchi
   with Sautéed Kale   221
Goat
Pam's Roast Goat with Figs & Herbs   143
Three Little Birds' Curry Goat   146
Goats' Cheese
   Goats' Cheese, Sausage and
     Pineapple Skewers   250
   Helen's Fig & Goats' Cheese Tart   72
   Sarah's Goats' Cheese with
     Cointreau Drizzle   148
   Golden Jubilee Ginger Log   254
   Golden Turmeric Latte   181
Grains
Sunny's Beetroot & Fennel Soup   71
Grandma Hora's Apple Shortcake   121
Grasshoppers, Fiona's Fried
   Grasshoppers with Satay Sauce   167
Gratin Buffalo Mozzarella Gratin   165
Green Chilli Sauce   136
Guinness Harry's Guinness Casserole   210

H
Harry's Guinness Casserole   210
Heather's Damson Paste   153
Helen's Fig & Goats' Cheese Tart   72
Herbs see also specific herbs
   Fleur's Cod & Cockles in a Kelp Bag   80
   Julie's Kelmarna Waiata Frittata   75
   Maureen's Asian Barbecue Trout   232
   Pam's Roast Goat with Figs
     & Herbs   143

Hinga's Pork Bones and Watercress
Boil-Up   208
Honey, Daphne's Mum's Mum's
   Honey Steamed Pudding   122

I
Icing, see Toppings
Infused Oil   59

J
Janet's Blue Cheesy Mushrooms   42
Janice's Seafood & Saffron Paella   91
Jason's Butcher's Pie   100
Jellied Pineapple   252
Jeremy's Salmon & Salsa Burgers   47
Jill's Seaweed & Carrot Loaf   222
Jo's Feijoa Self-Saucing Pudding   157
John's Mashpee Indian Clambake   86
Jools' One Egg Corn Fritters   129
Josje's Artichoke Gnocchi with
   Sautéed Kale   221
Julie's Kelmarna Waiata Frittata   75

K
Kale
   Josje's Artichoke Gnocchi with
     Sautéed Kale   221
   Sautéed Kale   221
Kefir, Organic Kefir   225
Kelp Chips   53
Kerry's Rosemary and Orange
   Lamb Marinade   37
Koura, Michelle's Koura with Pikopiko   231
Kumara, Hinga's Pork Bones &
   Watercress Boil-Up   208

L
Lamb, Linda's Oat-Crusted Roast   37
Lasagne, Tracey's Molesworth Chicken
Lasagne   213
Latte, Golden Turmeric Latte   181
Lavender, Carolyn's Lavender Cheesecake
   187
Lentils
   Annie's Duck Curry   111
   Libby's Delhi Dahl   173
Lime, Infused Oil   59
Linda's Oat-Crusted Roast   37
Loaves see Baking
Lynda's Duck Breast Paté   130
Lynley's Barbecue Chicken with
   Truffles   241

M
Mac's Turmeric Tarakihi   180
Mandarins
   Michelle's Koura with Pikopiko   231
   Wild Salad   53
Marg's Rump Curry with Naan Bread   62
Mariano's Ous Al Plat   23
Marinades, Kerry's Rosemary &
   Orange Lamb Marinade   37

Maureen's Asian Barbecue Trout   232
Michelle's Koura with Pikopiko   231
Milk
   Golden Turmeric Latte   181
   Organic Kefir   225
Mozzarella, Buffalo Mozzarella Gratin   165
Mushrooms
Dan Dan Sauce   177
Freddy's Dan Dan Noodles   177
Janet's Blue Cheesy Mushrooms   42
Mushroom & Green Peppercorn Sauce   138

N
Naan Bread   62
Nana's Bacon Balls   18
Nana's Gingernut Biscuits   126
Noodles, Freddy's Dan Dan Noodles   177
Nova's Flower Fritters   188

O
Oats
   Linda's Oat-Crusted Roast   37
   Nana's Bacon Balls   18
Oils, flavoured see Sauces
Oranges
   Kerry's Rosemary & Orange
     Lamb Marinade   37
   Pam's Roast Goat with Figs &
     Herbs   143
Organic Kefir   225
Ostrich, Rosemary's Ostrich Steak
   & Egg Burgers   163

P
Paella see Rice
Pam's Roast Goat with Figs & Herbs   143
Pancakes, Carolann's Blueberry
   Buttermilk Pancakes   154
Parsley
   Creamy Caper & Gherkin Sauce   138
   Phil's Mum's Stuffed Turkey   109
Pasta, Tracey's Molesworth
   Chicken Lasagne   213
Paste, Heather's Damson Paste   153
Pastry, Rough Puff Pastry   119
Paté, Lynda's Duck Breast Paté   130
Paua, Cream Paua Filling   200
Peaches, Harry's Guinness Casserole   210
Peanuts
   Peanut Sauce   136
   Satay Sauce   167
Pears
   Pear & Blackberry Sauce   138
   Wild Salad   53
Peppercorns, Mushroom & Green
   Peppercorn Sauce   138
Pheasant
   Bridgette's Pheasant Pies   119
   Pheasant Stock   119
Phil's Mum's Stuffed Turkey   109
Pies
Bridgette's Pheasant Pies   119

Jason's Butcher's Pie 100
Pikopiko, Michelle's Koura with
Pikopiko 231
Pineapple
Annie's Duck Curry 111
Goats' Cheese, Sausage &
Pineapple Skewers 250
Jellied Pineapple 252
John's Mashpee Indian Clambake 86
Pine nuts, Sautéed Silverbeet 210
Potatoes
Hinga's Pork Bones & Watercress
Boil-Up 208
Josje's Artichoke Gnocchi with
Sautéed Kale 221
Pork
Anna's Brine Pork Roast 26
Dan Dan Sauce 177
Freddy's Dan Dan Noodles 177
Hinga's Pork Bones & Watercress
Boil-Up 208
Pudding
Daphne's Mum's Mum's Honey
Steamed Pudding 122
Jo's Feijoa Self-Saucing Pudding 157
Pumpkin, Tracey's Molesworth
Chicken Lasagne 213

R
Raspberry Icing 191
Rice, Janice'ss Seafood & Saffron
Paella 91
Roses
Crystallised Rose Petals 191
Ruth's English Rose Cake 191
Rose water
Rose Cream 191
Rose Syrup 191
Ruth's English Rose Cake 191
Rosemary
Kerry's Rosemary & Orange Lamb
Marinade 37
Infused Oil 59
Pear & Blackberry Sauce 138
Rosemary's Ostrich Steak &
Egg Burgers 163
Rough Puff Pastry 119
Ruth's English Rose Cake 191

S
Saffron, Janice's Seafood & Saffron
Paella 91
Salads, Wild Salad 53
Salmon
Bruce's Cold Smoked Salmon 48
Frank's Crab Apple Salmon with
Kelp Chips 53
Jeremy's Salmon & Salsa Burgers 47
Salsas see Sauces
Sarah's Goats' Cheese with Cointreau
Drizzle 148
Satay Sauce 167

Sauces
Apple Sauce 134
Avocado Salsa 47
Brandy Sauce 59
Cheese Fondue 136
Creamy Caper & Gherkin Sauce 138
Dan Dan Sauce 177
Felicity's Feijoa Salsa for Wild Game
Meat 235
Green Chilli Sauce 136
Infused Oil 59
Mushroom & Green Peppercorn
Sauce 138
Peanut Sauce 136
Satay Sauce 167
Spicy Hollandaise Sauce 134
Tanah's La You Chilli Oil 174
Tzatziki 134
Sauces, sweet
Cointreau Drizzle 148
Pear & Blackberry Sauce 138
Rose Syrup 191
Whipped Coconut Cream 136
Sausages
Bangers in Cauliflower 254
Goats' Cheese, Sausage &
Pineapple Skewers 250
Scotch Eggs 252
Sautéed Kale 221
Sautéed Silverbeet 210
Seaweed
Fleur's Cod & Cockles in a Kelp Bag 80
Jill's Seaweed & Carrot Loaf 222
John's Mashpee Indian Clambake 86
Kelp Chips 53
Shellfish see also specific shellfish
Janice's Seafood & Saffron Paella 91
John's Mashpee Indian Clambake 86
Shortcake, Grandma Hora's Apple
Shortcake 121
Silverbeet
Sautéed Silverbeet 210
Tracey's Molesworth Chicken
Lasagne 213
Skewers, Goats' Cheese, Sausage &
Pineapple Skewers 250
Soups, Sunny's Beetroot & Fennel
Soup 71
Spicy Hollandaise Sauce 134
Spreads on Bread 250
Stocks
Duck Stock 111
Pheasant Stock 119
Sultanas, Daphne's Mum's Mum's
Honey Steamed Pudding 122
Sunny's Beetroot & Fennel Soup 71
Syrups see Sauces, sweet

T
Tarakihi, Mac's Turmeric Tarakihi 180
Tanah's La You Chilli Oil 174
Tarragon, Spicy Hollandaise Sauce 134

Tarts, Helen's Fig & Goats' Cheese Tart 72
Tash's Fry Bread 200
Three Little Birds' Curry Goat 146
Tim's Barbecued Backstrap with
Brandy Sauce 59
Tomatoes
Janet's Blue Cheesy Mushrooms 42
Toppings
Crystallised Rose Petals 191
Raspberry Icing 191
Rose Cream 191
Tracey's Molesworth Chicken Lasagne 213
Trout, Maureen's Asian Barbecue
Trout 232
Truffles, Lynley's Barbecue Chicken
with Truffles 241
Turkey, Phil's Mum's Stuffed Turkey 109
Turmeric
Golden Turmeric Latte 181
Libby's Delhi Dahl 173
Mac's Turmeric Tarakihi 180
Three Little Birds' Curry Goat 146
Tzatziki 134

V
Vegetables see also specific vegetables
Julie's Kelmarna Waiata Frittata 75
Venison
Marg's Rump Curry with Naan
Bread 62
Tim's Barbecued Backstrap with
Brandy Sauce 59

W
Walnuts
Janet's Blue Cheesy Mushrooms 42
Wild Salad 53
Watercress
Hinga's Pork Bones & Watercress
Boil-Up 208
Wild Salad 53
Whipped Coconut Cream 136
Wild Salad 53

Y
Yoghurt
Ruth's English Rose Cake 191
Scotch Eggs 252
Tzatziki 134

Z
Zucchini, Jools' One Egg Corn Fritters 129

ACKNOWLEDGEMENTS

We wish to thank all those who have contributed to the *Topp Country* book, especially our amazing food producers who generously agreed to be filmed and shared their stories, passion and home recipes with us.

A big thank you to all New Zealand's ethical farmers and growers who are committed to making our food healthier and tastier and leaving our land more productive for the next generation of foodies.

Finely, thanks to our awesome creative team and photographers, especially the Diva gals, Arani and MIchelle, who drove this project.

PRODUCER: Arani Cuthbert
DESIGN: Debbie Dale, Michelle Duff, Vince McMillan and Yolanta Woldendorp
PRE-PRESS: Jason Creaghan
PRODUCTION MANAGER: Michelle Duff
SUB-EDITOR: Siana Clifford
Cover Design: Olivia Tuck
Production: Sally McIntosh
ADDITIONAL RECIPES: Felicity Morgan-Rhind, Pip Wylie

www.toppcountry.com
Find and follow the Topp Twins on

PHOTO CREDITS

Front Cover - Sally Tagg/Women's Day
Back Cover Images - Arani Cuthbert
Inside Front Cover - Arani Cuthbert
Pg 4 - Sally Tagg/Women's Day
Pg 6 - Felicity Morgan-Rhind
Pg 7 - Topp Family Private Collection, Freddy Castro/unsplash
Pg 11 - Sally Tagg/Women's Day
Pg 12 - Peter Malloy
PORK
Pg 15, 16, 17, 18, 19, 22, 24, 25, 28 – Arani Cuthbert
Pg 20, 21, 23, 25 Mahy Family – Felicity Morgan-Rhind
SHEEP
Pg 31, 32, 33, 36 - Arani Cuthbert
Pg 34, 35 - John Burton, Landlife Images
Pg 38, 39, 40 - Michelle Duff
Pg 40-41 - Elizabeth Koroivulaono
Pg 40-41 Sheep Images – Paul McCredie
Pg 41 Miles & Janet King – MiNDFOOD/Jeff McEwan
Pg 43 - Felicity Morgan-Rhind
SALMON
Pg 44 - Bev Short
Pg 45 - Lynda Topp Private Collection
Pg 46 Richard & Margaret Logan – Margaret Logan
Pg 46, 49 - Arani Cuthbert
Pg 52 - Felicity Morgan-Rhind
Pg 54 - Sally Tagg/Diva Productions
Pg 55 - Arani Cuthbert/Diva Productions
VENISON
Pg 57, 58, 63, 64, 65 - Diva Productions
Pg 60-61 - Rob Suisted
www.naturespic.com

GARDEN
Pg 69-77 - Diva Productions (except vegetables & beetroot)
SEA
Pg 79, 82, 88, 89 (except Saffron field and threads), 90 - Diva Productions
Pg 81 - Ferne Smyth & Fleur Sullivan
Pg 82, 83, 84, 85 - John Panoho
Pg 87 - Michelle Duff
Pg 90 Paella - Elizabeth Koroivulaono
BEEF
Pg 93 - Topp Twins Private Collection
Pg 95 - Bruce Connew
Pg 98, 101, 102, 103, 104 & 105 - Diva Productions
Pg 101 Hororata Café - Jarnia Kupe
Pg 103 Taco - Jono Parker
POULTRY
Pg 107-113 - Diva Productions
HERITAGE
Pg 117, 120, 123 - Diva Productions
Pg 118 - Elizabeth Koroivulaono
Pg 120 Grandma Hora - Richard Bowman
Pg 121 - Sarah Bowman
TOPPS
Pg 124, 125 & 126 - Topp Family Private Collection
Pg 127, 128-131 - Diva Productions
Pg 128 Jools & Whitefeather - Jools Topp
Pg 128 Jools with Horses – Deb Filler
Pg 131 Topp Lodge - Lynda Topp
CAMP MOTHER & CAMP LEADER
Pg 132- 139 - Diva Productions
GOATS
Pg 141-143, 147-149 - Diva Productions
Pg 142 Family - Elizabeth Koroivulaono
Pg 144, 145 - Susie Hamilton

FRUIT
Pg 151-159 - Diva Productions
EXOTIC
Pg 161-164, 166, 167 - Diva Productions
Pg 165 - Felicity Morgan-Rhind
SPICE
Pg 171-178, 180, 182 - Diva Productions
Pg 179 - McGregor Smith
FLOWERS
Pg 185 - Topp Family Private Collection
Pg 186-190 - Diva Productions
Pg 193 - Topp Twins Private Collection
BREAD
Pg 196, 197, 199 - Deb Filler Private Collection
Pg 197, 200, 201 - Diva Productions
BACKYARD
Pg 204-208, 211, 216 - Diva Productions
Pg 212-214 - Elizabeth Koroivulaono
ORGANICS
Pg 219 - Huw Morgan
Pg 220, 222-224 - Diva Productions
BUSH
Pg 230-237 - Diva Productions
DECADENCE
Pg 240-247 - Diva Productions
BOWLING LADIES
Pg 248-255 - Diva Productions
THANKS
260, 261 Topp Country Crew - Diva Productions, Dana Devolk/unsplash

Inside Back Cover - Arani Cuthbert

All other images sourced from Getty Images

A HUGE THANK YOU...

goes out to our wonderful TV crew who helped craft the Topp Country series this book is based on. A special shout-out goes to our director, Felicity Morgan-Rhind, whose love of cooking, people and story-telling infused the show. We're also grateful to Clayton Carpinter, Richard Harling, Nigel Gordon-Crosby, Elizabeth Koroivulaono, Wayne Cook, Richard Shaw, Sacha Campbell, James Brookes and Department of Post, Nigel Foster and Post Production Sound, Michelle Duff and our producer Arani Cuthbert.

MICHELLE DUFF

FELICITY MORGAN-RHIND

ARANI CUTHBERT

ELIZABETH KOROIVULAONO

RICHARD HARLING AND CLAYTON CARPINTER

NIGEL GORDON-CROSBY

DEB FRAME

HAMISH WILSON

PETER YOUNG

WAYNE VINTEN

SHAUN LOGAN